On Pointe

On Pointe

Basic Pointe Work
Beginner — Low Intermediate
Thalia Mara

and

A Look at the USA International Ballet Competition
Janice Barringer

Princeton Book Company, Publishers
Hightstown, NJ

On Pointe

Basic Pointe Work, Beginner—Low Intermediate
and
A Look at the USA International Ballet Competition
by Thalia Mara and Janice Barringer

Basic Pointe Work, originally published as Fourth Steps in Ballet: On Your Toes!
Copyright © 1959 by Thalia Mara

A Look at the USA Inetrnational Ballet Competition
Copyright © 2005 by Janice Barringer and Leanne Mahoney
Foreword copyright © 2005 by Richard Philp

Line drawings by Louise Holmgren
Photographs of Sarah Lamb, used by permission of Rosalie O'Connor, photographer, were especially photographed for this book.
Photographs in A Look at the USA IBC used by permission of Hubert Worley, Official Photographer of the 1986, 1990, 1994 & 1998
USA IBC; Christopher Jean-Richard, Official Photographer of the 2002 USA IBC; Alexander Skalij; John F. Mahoney.
Photographs in Thalia Mara (1911-2003) are from the collection of Leanne Mahoney and are used by permission.

A Dance Horizons Book
Princeton Book Company, Publishers
PO Box 831
Hightstown, New Jersey

Interior design by Lisa Denham and John McMenamin
Cover design by John McMenamin

ISBN 0-87127-267-9

Library of Congress Cataloging in Publication Data
On pointe.
    p.cm.
  Contents: Basic pointe work: beginner-low intermediate / Thalia Mara -- A look at the
USA International Ballet Competiton / Janice Barringer.
  ISBN 0-87127-267-9 (alk. paper)
    1. Ballet dancing. 2. USA International Ballet Competition--History. I. Mara, Thalia. Fourth steps in ballet.
II. Mara, Thalia. Basic pointe work III. Barringer, Janice. Look at the USA International Ballet Competiton.
GV1788.O62 2005
792.8--dc22   2005048659

Printed in Canada   8, 7, 6, 5, 4, 3, 2, 1

Contents

Part 1
Basic Pointe Work, Beginner — Low Intermediate

FOREWORD	vii	GLISSADE ON POINTE	35
ACKNOWLEDGMENTS	ix	Glissade Changée	35
INTRODUCTION TO PART I	3	Glissade Changée with Small Développé	35
THE FOOT	7	PIQUÉ	37
THE CARE OF THE FEET AND POINTE SHOES	8	Piqué en Arrière, Coupé Dessus	37
The Care of the Feet	8	Piqué en Avant, Coupé Dessous	40
Pointe Shoes	9	Piqué en Arabesque Ouverte	42
Selecting and Preparing the Shoes	12	PAS DE BOURRÉE PIQUÉ	44
POSITION ON POINTE	14	PAS DE BOURRÉE COURU, EN CINQUIÈME	49
RELEVÉS	15	ASSEMBLÉ SOUTENU, ON POINTE	54
Relevé from Straight-Knee Positions	16	Dessus	54
Relevé from Demi-plié	19	Assemblé Soutenu with an Example of Port de Bras	55
ÉCHAPPÉ ON POINTE	23	Dessous	56
Échappé à la Seconde without Change of Feet	23	COUPÉ ON POINTE, FOUETTÉ RACCOURCI	57
Échappé en Croisé and Échappé Changé	24	BALLONNÉ ON POINTE	59
RELEVÉ FROM TWO FEET TO ONE FOOT	26	SISSONNE ON POINTE	61
Relevé Devant	26	Sissonne en Arabesque	61
Relevé Derrière	27	RELEVÉ ON ONE FOOT	63
Relevé Passé en Arrière	27	Relevé en Arabesque	63
Relevé Passé en Avant	28	Relevé en Attitude Croisé	64
Relevé Devant and Derrière with an Example of Port de Bras and Body Movement	29	EMBOÎTÉ ON POINTE	65
		DEMI-PLIÉ ON POINTE	67
Relevé Passé en Arrière with Port de Bras	31	SAUTÉ ON POINTE	69
Relevé Passé en Avant with Port de Bras	33	Sauté on pointe and Changement	69
		Pas de cheval	70
		Sautillé on pointe	71

Contents

Part II
A Look at the USA International Ballet Competition

INTRODUCTION TO PART II: HOW DOES A DANCER PREPARE
TO ENTER AN INTERNATIONAL BALLET COMPETITION?   75
  The Differences Between Competitions   77
  International Ballet Competitions   79
  Other Major Competitions   80

WHAT IS THE
USA INTERNATIONAL BALLET COMPETITION?   83

HISTORY OF THE
USA INTERNATIONAL BALLET COMPETITION   84
  An Idea is Conceived   84
  Jackson is Chosen   85
  Distinguished Participants   88
  An Angel Appears   88

HOW THE COMPETITION IS ORGANIZED   89
  The Staff   89
  The Competition Program   89
  How the Jury Judges a Competitor   91

REQUIREMENTS FOR ENTRY   93

AWARDS, HOUSING, HOSPITALITY AND HOST FAMILIES   94

BALLET INSTRUCTION AT THE COMPETITION   95
  The International Dance School   95
  Teachers' Course   96
  Residencies and Other Workshops   96
  Jackson's Special Features   96

THE COMPETITION EXPERIENCE   97
  Danny Tidwell, Joseph Phillips, April Ball and Simon Ball,
    William Starrett, José Manuel Carreño,
    Katia Carranza and Luis Serrano,
    Agnes Oaks and Thomas Edur
  Katherine Healy Remembers   104
  Audiences   108
  Coaches   108

ADVICE FROM MEDALISTS TO FUTURE COMPETITORS   110
  Rasta Thomas, José Manuel Carreño, Sarah Lamb,
    Danny Tidwell, Joseph Phillips, Katherine Healy

THALIA MARA (1911-2003)   113

AUTHORS AND CONTRIBUTORS   127

Foreword

When the Jackson (Mississippi) City Council rechristened the Jackson Municipal Auditorium, a monumental performing space of some 2,400 seats, as Thalia Mara Hall (in 1986), it was renamed in honor of a monumental pioneer in twentieth-century American dance. Teacher, writer, educator, performer, philosopher, historian, and advocate, Thalia's accomplishments in ballet were astonishing to many of us who at first wondered and watched from afar as she brought the first international ballet competition in the United States to Jackson. Her life before Jackson had been equally impressive, if not more so. The reissue of her book *Fourth Steps in Ballet: On Your Toes!* (retitled *On Pointe*) by Princeton Book Company, Publishers, renews one of her most lasting legacies—her careful and anatomically-grounded teaching methods, which have produced some of the most prominent artists in the galaxy of stars in dance today.

The formation of the USA International Ballet Competition (known fondly as the IBC) was a new chapter in assisting in the maturation of young ballet dancers seeking enhanced experience in a very difficult and competitive profession. Providing young dancers with some of the necessary experience to face their futures may turn out to be Thalia's most important legacy during the last twenty years of her life.

One of the most significant aspects of the IBC's evolution was the introduction, for the first time ever at such an event, of a psychological safety net of support, as well as sensitive guidance to those competing dancers who did not place in the ranks of "winners." I use the word *winners* with circumspection because a young dancer's qualifying for Jackson and going through the ordeal of competing with other major talent created many more winners than you will find in the impressive listing of those who actually won prizes.

Young dancers going to the IBC, held every four years, can gain enormous experience through working with some of today's best teachers and from coming in contact with prominent professionals in their chosen field; not to mention the distinct advantages of making new friends from around the world. One of my great sources of knowledge and inspiration, Marian Horosko, herself an excellent teacher and inspiring author of many dance books, first brought Mara's beautifully written and clearly illustrated books to my attention in 1970 at *Dance Magazine*, where I became editor-in-chief.

Marian told me that I should become familiar with Thalia's books because they contained the best and most reliable text on the mysteries of ballet technique. They quickly became indispensable to me as an editor. My team of proofreaders, fact checkers, writers, and I referred to Thalia's books often over many years, undoubtedly contributing to the well-deserved reputation for accuracy we managed to maintain at the magazine.

What a pleasure it was for me to meet this great lady in 1989, when she asked me to serve as chairman of the IBC's International Advisory Committee! It turned out, to my delight, to be not just an honorary position, but a working one as well. The IBC these days is arguably the most prestigious of the world's ballet competitions.

The book that you are now holding in your hands is enhanced by the editing of Janice Barringer, who is herself the co-author of *The Pointe Book: Shoes, Training and Technique*, one of the most widely read books in the field. Janice has also contributed a fascinating essay, "A Look at the USA International Ballet Competition." Reading over this material, you will find that Thalia's friends and associates included men and women who were seminal to the expansion and development of dance in the twentieth century. To name only a few on a breathtaking list: Assaf Messerer, Natalia Dudinskaya, Yuri Grigorovich, Anton Dolin, Olga Preobrajenska (with whom Thalia studied in Paris and credits as her most important teacher), Michel Fokine, and Pepo (her parrot and companion for forty-five years). Her husband, Arthur Mahoney, was her dancing partner as well as her partner in founding and running her schools.

Thalia's basic principles are as sound as ever; so much of her advice is as valid today as it ever was. "A well-trained ballet teacher," she writes, "understands [the physiological development of bones in the feet] because knowledge of anatomy is a prerequisite for anyone who deals with the physical development of the body." As many of us have observed, "Deformed toes, painful bunion joints, or a nagging backache for life can be the result of incorrect training at too early an age."

Professional dancers, students, teachers, educators, historians, and audience members seeking to understand more about this beloved art form will find these pages of enduring value. Read on…

Richard Philp

Acknowledgments

Because every detail of past International Ballet Competitions in Jackson could not be listed, I have selected certain highlights that are intended to give the reader real insight into the competition and its workings.

While many people involved in the USA IBC have been mentioned by name, it is impossible and cumbersome to list everyone. I have not meant to slight anyone who has not been mentioned, since all of these wonderful people have made enormous contributions to the success of the competition.

Much of the information in the biography of Thalia Mara was drawn from an interview and article for the *Clarion Ledger* (12/27/83), written by Leslie R. Myers of Jackson.

Information on the history and rules and regulations has been culled from the IBC 25th Anniversary Reunion Gala program and the IBC website. But, by far, most has been obtained by personal interviews of Ms. Mara's family, close friends and associates, competition competitors and others closely associated with either Ms. Mara or the USA IBC.

I am very grateful to Leanne Mahoney, William Mounger, Bruce Marks, Randolph Swartz, Donald Saddler, Genevieve Oswald, David Howard, Olga Smoak, Jolinda Menendez, William Starrett, Katherine Healy, Thomas Edur, Agnes Oaks, José Manuel Carreño, Simon Ball, April Ball, Rasta Thomas, Luis Serrano, Wu Haiyan, Mikhail Ilyin, Katia Carranza, Joseph Phillips and Danny Tidwell for providing me with personal reflections, insights, information and advice. Additional thanks to Dee Mangold for digital scan of photography and to Nicole Bradshaw and Sue Lobrano.

Special thanks go to Sarah Lamb for agreeing to be photographed for the first part of this book. I am very grateful to the Royal Ballet for letting us use the Kenneth MacMillan Studio for the photo shoot.

Let me not forget to say how grateful I am to my husband, Rick, a businessman who listens to endless discussion on ballet, and who also is content to have me leave him for long periods of time for my research.

Last, but certainly not least, a big thank you to Rosalie O'Connor, an extraordinary dance photographer, for traveling with me to London, and also for helping both Sarah and me with her expertise in ballet and photography.

Janice Barringer

1
Basic Pointe Work
Beginner - Low Intermediate

Thalia Mara

Introduction to Part 1
Basic Pointe Work
Beginner — Low Intermediate

Dancing on pointe is part of the art of academic classical ballet. It is the ultimate in technical attainment for the female ballet dancer.

Although the art of ballet is some four hundred years old, dancing on the tips of the toes did not come into being until the early part of the nineteenth century. It is believed that it was invented by Philippe Taglioni for his daughter Marie, one of the greatest ballerinas of her day.

The purpose of rising to the ends of the toes was to give a quality of lightness and ethereality to the dance. The romantic ballet was born in the 1830's, and use of the pointes in dancing helped to convey a feeling of supernatural lightness and an "out of this world" quality to the dancers who were portraying wraiths, sylphs, and wilis in such ballets as *La Sylphide* and *Giselle.*

Early dancers such as Marie Taglioni, Fanny Cerrito, Lucille Grahn, and Carlotta Grisi, all of whom were famed exponents of the romantic ballet, wore unblocked slippers – that is, their slippers were not stiffened at the toes – but achieved some measure of support by darning the ends of the slippers. They did not, of course, perform the very difficult technical feats that ballerinas today are called upon to do, but were content with a few simple *relevés* and *piqués.*

The acrobatic qualities of dancing on pointe seemed to have caught the fancy of the music-hall public early in the twentieth century. This phase of ballet technique soon degenerated into vulgar displays of acrobatic tricks, even up to the point of "tap on toe" and vaudeville acts in which girls jumped rope and tapped up and down flights of stairs on pointe.

3

Children are fascinated by dancing on pointe, believing it to be the epitome of glamour. Every little girl who studies dance dreams of dancing on her toes.

Actually, the only children who should dance on pointe are those who are training for a professional career in ballet. The training is rigorous and requires several years of intensive technical training to develop muscular strength in the back, the thighs, and the insteps prior to this difficult and advanced stage of development. Most children who do not plan to enter the profession do not have the time or the inclination to devote the hours of work required.

However, since I am aware that thousands of youngsters will continue to demand toe shoes from their ballet teachers, it is my purpose in this book to set forth, as clearly as possible, the correct aspects of the technical training in the hope that it will help to clear up some popular misconceptions and to correct some evils that exist through bad and careless teaching.

Parents, seeing a beautiful ballerina on stage or television, are convinced that a year or two of study will give their daughters the posture, the poise, and the grace of the dancers. And so hundreds of thousands of children are enrolled annually in dancing schools. This would be wonderful if there were enough good teachers to meet this popular demand, or if parents were so informed about ballet that they would demand the proper kind of training. Unfortunately, this is not the case. There are many teachers who profess to teach ballet but who do not possess the necessary background of training to undertake safely the training of others, particularly young children. These circumstances lead to actual physical damage to the feet, knees and backs of many children.

One of the greatest evils committed by poor teachers is the pointe lessons which they give to physically unprepared children and children who are entirely too young to learn this form of dancing with safety.

Doctors will tell you that the bones of the toes are the last bones of the foot to be developed. Up to the age of sixteen years these bones, and many others of the foot, are really cartilage similar to that of the nose or the ear. It is not until after the tenth year that these soft and malleable bones begin to harden; prior to this time the feet cannot take the strain and stress of pointe work without injury or even deformity.

A well-trained ballet teacher understands this because knowledge of anatomy is a prerequisite for anyone who deals with the physical development of the body. In professional schools that train children for the ballet stage, the children are carefully watched and nurtured in the development of their training.

Training in academic technique does not begin before the age of eight, and several years are spent in technical exercises that develop the needed strength and muscle tone.

Ballet exercises are soundly scientific. When correctly administered they build a beautiful, sound, symmetrical body. Since the feet are so important in ballet, its exercises are so planned that they remake the feet into instruments of dance – they become strong, extremely supple, and sensitive. Under proper teaching and careful supervision pointe dancing will not be harmful.

No child should begin before the age of ten, nor without several years of training in soft slippers. Ballet training should consist not only of learning dances and combinations but should stress academic exercises.

The teacher, alone, should determine when the child is ready to begin pointe training. The decision will be based on the child's response to the training, on her weight, strength, ability, and muscle tone. As can be readily seen, this will vary with each student.

Correct placement determines the readiness of the student. Preliminary training in ballet is concerned primarily with the posture; to develop the strength of the postural muscles of the back, for it is these muscles that give control of the body to the dancer. No student should attempt pointe work until perfect posture is part of her being. When the dancer can stand straight, with the head in proper alignment to the spine, rise to the *demi-pointe* (the balls of the feet) maintaining this perfect alignment as well as tightly pulled-up knees and body weight lifted from the feet, pulled up and distributed through the body, she is ready to begin the study of pointe work.

It is my earnest hope that every parent of every child who studies ballet will realize that pointe shoes should not be given as a Christmas present to a child who is not prepared to use them properly; that it is not the case that the teacher is just being mean and needs to be cajoled into letting Susie (who is just dying to get up on her toes) have her way, because her friend Melissa, who studies in that other dancing school, got her pointe shoes right away.

Deformed toes, painful bunion joints, and nagging backaches for life are the result of incorrect training at too early an age. Forewarned is forearmed!

Thalia Mara

The Foot

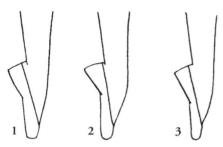

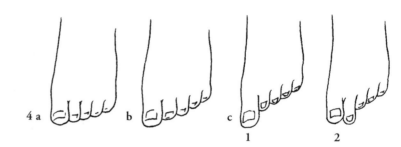

1. The ideal foot for dancing *sur les pointes* is the square foot – one that gives the impression that the toes are sawed off straight across – with a low arch and a solid, strong ankle. Such a foot will wear well and will be a great comfort to the dancer because in standing on pointe the weight of the body will be borne evenly by all of the toes.

2. This foot, while more beautiful in appearance because of its high arch (beginning almost in the ankle) and its slim, well-turned ankle, is much more difficult to work with because of its great flexibility and softness. Even with excellent training and care it will never be as strong as the foot illustrated in Figure 1. Dancers with this type of foot must be especially careful in their training and must go through a longer preparatory period before attempting to dance on pointe.

3. Another type of high arch; this one, however, is stronger than the foot illustrated in Figure 2, because the arch does not involve the ankle joint.

4. The grouping of the toes is very important to the would-be ballet dancer: a. short toes, all even in length, are the best for pointe work because all the toes will share the burden of the dancer's weight; b. at least three toes should be "carriers"; c. 1 and 2. when one toe is longer than the rest the dancer finds toe work difficult and painful.

The Care of the Feet and Pointe Shoes

REVISED AND UPDATED BY JANICE BARRINGER

THE CARE OF THE FEET

With a reasonable amount of care your feet will be none the worse for dancing on the tips of your toes, *provided that you are properly prepared physically* when you begin this phase of ballet technique.

The skin of the toes and the entire foot should be kept dry, soft, and pliant at all times. It should not be allowed to dry out so that it cracks, or to become moist and tender so that it rubs off, blisters, or forms soft corns between the toes.

A good practice to follow is a nightly massage with a bit of Vaseline after the feet are bathed and thoroughly dried. Be sure to dry well between the toes, then rub a tiny amount of Vaseline into the skin of the toes, working it in until it disappears. Push a little into the space around the toenails with an orangewood stick to prevent the formation of calluses between the nail and the skin, particularly in the big toes. Pay special attention to the skin on the heels at the back so that it does not become dry and cracked. During the massage, take hold of each toe individually, pull it and stretch it a little, and move it around. Knead the metatarsal arch with the thumb, particularly around the big-toe joint. Wipe off any excess Vaseline; do not leave the feet greasy. Consistent daily care of this sort will pay off with skin that is soft and pliant and that does not rub off easily or blister or crack.

Inevitably, if you dance long enough and advance to the point where you do many difficult things and where you spend many hours dancing on pointe, you will have occasion to deal with blisters and rubbed toes. One way to deal with this condition is to use "New Skin," a commercial preparation that can be bought in the drugstore and that puts a protective coating over the raw spot until the skin can grow over it again. Follow the directions on the package if you use this preparation. Another way to cope with a blister or rubbed toe is to put a dab of boric-acid ointment on the raw spot, after using a little iodine or disinfectant on it. Then cover it well with a waterproof adhesive bandage. Change the dressing daily and do not allow the affected toe to get wet.

The toenails must be kept short for dancing on pointe. Long toenails will bruise and cause the feet to feel very sore. If there is a tendency toward ingrown toenails, cut the nail a little shorter in the center like the letter U. Students are sometimes alarmed when they develop a toenail that thickens and grows off, but this need not bother anyone. It is usually the result of a bruise or of pressure on that particular toe. A nail that grows off is always replaced by a new one growing underneath the old one.

If there is a good podiatrist or chiropodist in your area, it is a good idea to visit him or her periodically to check over your feet and nails.

For those students who have one toe longer than the others there will always be a problem. If the condition is not too marked, the dancer can sometimes learn to work with it. In this case it is helpful to wrap the longer toe in a little lamb's wool under the tights. There are a variety of gel products on the market manufactured specifically to alleviate the pain of pointe work. If, however, one toe is much longer than any of the others, the student will find it impossible to dance on pointe because the condition will always cause a great deal of pain.

POINTE SHOES

In order to dance well, the dancer must wear the correct shoes, and these must be properly fitted to the feet.

Unfortunately there are very wide popular misconceptions concerning toe shoes – their construction, their fitting, and their care.

Until very recently, the properly made shoe has always been hand-sewn, but currently some are machine made. The cost and man hours involved in such a time-consuming process has been the reason for this change in the way pointe shoes are made. The shoes should be very lightly boxed or blocked (the hard portion at the end of the shoe), and must be completely flexible and light in weight. The dancer should investigate thoroughly before purchasing her pointe shoes as recently many are made with harder glue or even pre-constructed boxes that are definitely not light. The reason for this change has been to extend the life of the shoes because of the expense of having to replace shoes frequently when they wear out. The shoe should fit the foot like a glove so that it does not impede the dancer's movements.

The use of stiff, hard, heavy shoes stems from the fact that there is so much poor and careless teaching of ballet. A student who has been improperly prepared for pointe work lacks muscle tone and the necessary strength in the feet, thighs, and back to support herself in standing on the tips of the toes. Therefore, there is the necessity for a shoe that is constructed so strongly that it will support the wearer's entire weight. In other words, since the dancer lacks the trained strength to support herself, the manufacturers of ballet shoes, in addition to wanting to make shoes last longer, have endeavored to help her by producing shoes that will do the work she should be doing herself.

The drawback here is that shoes of this weight and stiffness make it impossible for the dancer to use her feet properly.

At all times the dancer must have control of her feet for balance, and the ability to move freely and with ease depends on this. This is just as true for toe shoes as for soft ballet shoes. The dancer must be able to feel the floor with her toes, must be able to use the *demi-pointe* level of the foot as freely as the full-pointe level. Without the ability to use the *demi-pointe*, the dancer's movements must, of necessity, be jerky and hard because she will have to jump off her toes instead of rolling down smoothly.

From the very beginning the dancer must be trained on the correct shoes. Once dependence on hard, stiff shoes has been established, it is very difficult, sometimes impossible, to make the change to the correct, light shoes because it means learning a completely new way of dancing on the pointe.

The correct shoe may not be easy to find, particularly for those living in a small community. The shoes are worth searching for, and your dancing teacher can order them for you directly from the manufacturer or from a variety of catalogs.

The proper fitting of the shoes is vitally important. Pointe shoes must fit the feet snugly. They should not be bought large enough to grow into; *they must be bought for the present time*. This is absolutely necessary for two reasons: the protection of the feet and the aesthetic appearance. Shoes that are too large may easily cause the wearer to fall or to sprain the ankle or forefoot, because there can be no balance in shoes that are too large. They will look ugly because they will not conform to the dancer's foot as she points. Again, the shoe should fit the foot like a glove so that it bends and shapes with the movements of the foot.

Like all ballet shoes, toe shoes are normally fitted shorter than street shoes. This may be anywhere from one to two sizes shorter and one width wider than street shoes. Unfortunately, there is no consistency among the manufacturers when it comes to sizing. In trying on the shoes one should stand firmly on both feet. The ends of the toes should touch the end wall of the shoe with the toes stretched out straight. If the toes are pushed back so that they are forced to curl up slightly, the shoes are too short. One should have to tug a little to get the shoes on; they should not slip on and off like bedroom slippers. The width must be watched carefully, for the dancer must have freedom to move the foot – it must not be held as though in a vise.

When standing on pointe, there should be no gap at the sides of the shoes – such a gap means that it is too large.

The length of the shoe's vamp must be determined by the length of the dancer's toes. A long-toed foot requires a longer vamp than a short-toed foot. This is most important, for a difference as little as one-eighth of an inch in the length of the vamp can alter the dancer's position on pointe. If the vamp is too short, it will cause the foot to break over at the toes, making it extremely ugly. If, on the other hand, the vamp is too long, it will throw the dancer back and prevent her from attaining a full-pointe position.

The ideal thing that should be used inside the slippers to protect the toes is a little lamb's wool – very little! Currently, there are other products on the market that have about the same effect. The sole purpose of using this wool is to protect the skin of the toes from rubbing. Later, as the skin toughens up, the use of the wool can be entirely discontinued.

There is a horrible practice among some students – the use of rubbery, thick pads that surround the toes. Nothing could be worse for the feet, to say nothing of the fact that it is almost impossible to dance well when wearing them. First, the shoes will have to be worn several sizes too large in order to accommodate the pads. Second, some of these pads make the feet perspire profusely; this makes the skin tender, causing it to crack and rub off and forming soft corns and blisters. The feet must be kept as dry as possible for good health reasons as well as good dancing reasons. Third, the wearer of these pads has absolutely no contact with the floor; therefore she has no sure footing and no balance.

One should never be afraid to dance in soft shoes. When the boxing at the toes softens up sufficiently to permit the dancer to feel the floor, the dancer is able to do her best work. This is what is meant by "breaking in" a pair of pointe shoes. When putting on a pair of new shoes for the first time, it will help to soften them up so that they conform and mold to the movements of the feet more easily. This may be done by taking each shoe individually, grasping it firmly in one hand, and kneading it gently with the heel of the other hand all over the boxes.

With the exception of one shoe which is made in a completely different way, no pointe shoe will last forever. Naturally, the more advanced the dancer and the more work done in the shoes, the quicker they will wear out. Since this can become an expensive factor in your dance studies, here are some tips for preserving the life of your shoes:

- Keep two pairs in use at the same time, using them alternately in order to permit each pair to dry out thoroughly between uses.

- Never wet the backs of the heels of the shoes with water, as so many students do, in order to keep the shoe from slipping off at the heel. The water opens the pores of the leather, robbing it of its life and resiliency. Also, since the boxing at the toe end is normally made of layers of glue, the water will destroy the glue and cause the shoe to lose its shape and every vestige of support. (A dab of glue on the heel of your tights or an elastic loop such as illustrated in Figure 9 will keep your shoe on better.)

- After use, fold your shoes up neatly, wrap them in a clean towel, and keep them in a dry place in your practice bag, separate from your damp practice clothes. As soon as possible, take them out of the practice bag and open them up, allowing them to air thoroughly until the next time they are used.

Selecting And Preparing The Shoes

In selecting your shoes look for the following:

5. The satin of the pointe shoe is normally gathered into pleats on the underside of the shoes just as it is in soft ballet shoes. These pleats are important, for they provide for the expansion and movement of the toes. Incidentally, the presence of these pleats is your proof that the shoe is hand-constructed.

6. The box should be light in weight.

7. The sole of the shoe must be flexible to permit the use of the *demi-pointe*. If the sole is very thick at the toe end and too stiff to permit the shoe to bend in this fashion, it is not the proper kind of shoe, for it will not permit the correct use of the feet.

In preparing the shoes for use, note these suggestions:

8. To find the correct place on which to sew the ribbons, bend the back of the shoe down until it touches the inner sole. Sew the end of the ribbon at the fold, attaching it to the canvas inner lining about midway between the binding and the sole. Do not stitch through the satin and do not sew to the binding, for the drawstring must remain free. The ribbon should be from three quarters of an inch to one inch in width. About one inch of the end of the ribbon should be folded under before it is sewn to the shoe in order to make the attachment strong and to eliminate any raveling. Sew the ribbon on with heavy thread, using cross-stitches. Clip the ends on the bias or singe with a match to prevent fraying.

9. An elastic loop sewn to the inside back of the heel will help to keep the shoes on at the heels, if one has trouble with this.

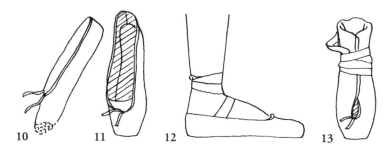

10. 11. 12. 13.

10. Darning helps to preserve the shoe for longer use because it prevents the satin from fraying. While darning the entire tip of the shoe is very effective, in recent times other methods have replaced this time-consuming chore. Darning the edge of the platform, though, is a method that is still in use. A more common and quicker way to make the shoe last longer is by apply Jet Glue to the outside and inside of the tip.

11. If you find that the vamp is too short and that you break across the toes as you stand on pointe, sew a piece of strong, heavy ribbon across the top of the vamp at the inside. While it's hard to find, vamp elastic (a very wide elastic that is more easily found in England) also works very well.

12. To properly tie a shoe, the ribbons must be straight (and clean!), not rolled up in strings. Tie a secure knot and tuck the ends of the ribbons out of sight. Draw the drawstrings, tie them securely (a box is best so that they can be readjusted easily) and tuck them inside under the vamp.

13. Put your shoes away carefully if you want them to last. Fold the back in to the inner sole, fold both sides over, wrap the ribbons around and tuck the ends in.

14. DON'T DO THIS!

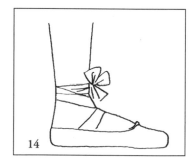

14

Position On Pointe

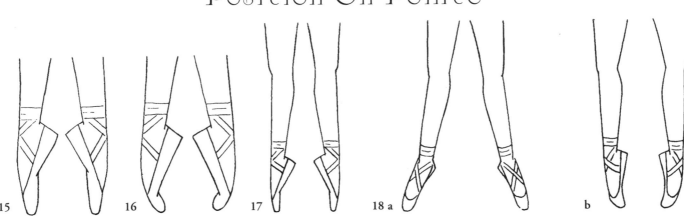

15   16   17   18 a   b

CORRECT POSITION

15. In standing correctly on pointe, the dancer stands on the pads of the toes pulling the weight upward from them as much as possible.

INCORRECT POSITION

16. Never push down on the toes, curling them over so that you stand on the knuckles.

CORRECT POSITION

17. The foot must be in its proper alignment when standing on pointe. Toes must be aligned to heel, and foot must be aligned to leg.

INCORRECT POSITION

18. a. Sickle in

    b. Sickle out

The arch must be developed through strength, not weakness. To achieve this strength, the dancer must be constantly pulling up through the insteps, not pushing down when standing on pointe. Do not press down on the feet so that they bear the weight of the body and you dance on your knuckles, as in Figure 16, but pull the weight of the body upward to take as much of it as possible off the toes. This develops the insteps correctly, giving them strength and stability.

Relevés

There are two correct ways to *relevé* — that is, to rise from the whole foot, with the heel firmly planted on the floor, to the full-pointe position. One is to roll up through the instep, keeping the toes in their original place and lifting the heel up through the ankle. The other is to lift the heel with a slight spring, at the same time drawing the toes slightly under. Both ways are useful.

We rise up, rolling through the instep, when we *relevé* from a straight-knee position; and we spring up, drawing the toes under the instep, when we relevé from a demi-plié.

Generally, rising from a straight knee is used for extremely quick and brilliant passages, such as are found in some of the old classical ballets.

It is wise for beginners to start their practice with these rising *relevés*, working with straight knees throughout and taking them very slowly and carefully in very exact positions.

In coming down from the pointes always roll down the instep passing through the *demi-pointe* before the heel touches the floor. This is most important, for it is this control through the insteps that makes your movements light and soft.

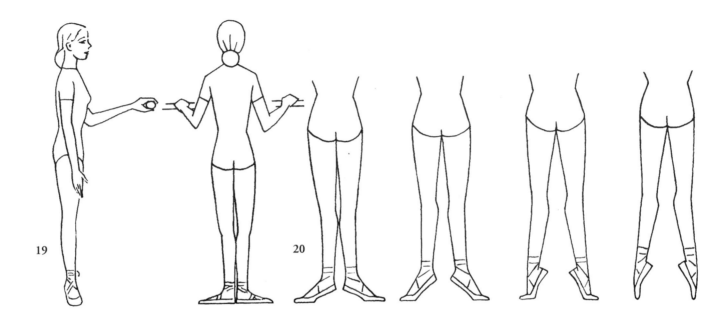

19   20

RELEVÉ FROM STRAIGHT-KNEE POSITIONS

19. Correct stance. Stand in First Position with perfect posture, correctly placed and well centered, with the weight of the body over the toes. The heels are held firmly to the floor, but they do not bear the weight of the body. Chin up, look straight out! Try not to lean on the barre as you *relevé* but rise up through the strength of your insteps, thighs, and back.

20. Rise to the quarter-pointe, the demi-pointe, the three-quarter pointe, and the full pointe, slowly, pulling up strongly through the knees and thighs and tightening the buttocks. Do not move the feet or permit the heels to twist back. Press the heels forward and do not sickle in or out on the ankles. Roll down slowly, exactly as you rose, coming down gently through each level of the feet.

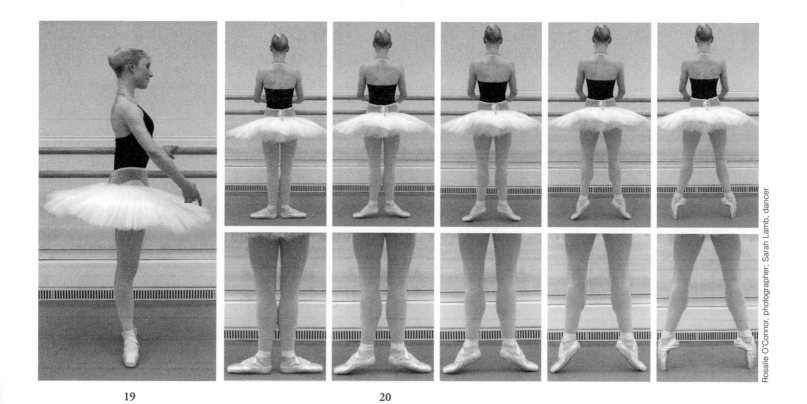

19

20

Rosalie O'Connor, photographer; Sarah Lamb, dancer

21. The same *relevés* performed in Second Position.

22. The same *relevés* performed in Open Fourth Position (Fourth Position out of First Position).

23. The same *relevés* performed in Crossed Fourth Position (Fourth Position out of Fifth Position).

24. The same *relevés* performed in Fifth Position.

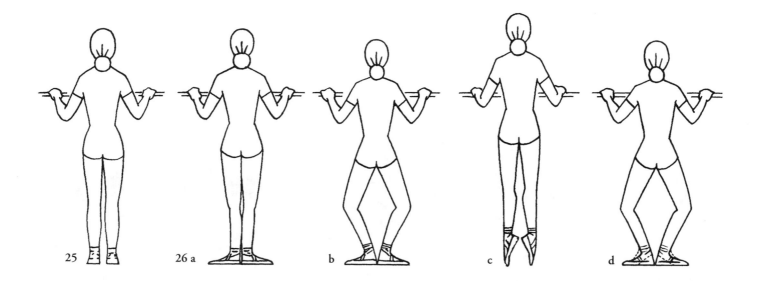

RELEVÉ FROM DEMI-PLIÉ

25. Face the barre and hold it firmly with both hands. Be sure that your posture is good and your placement correct. Remember that your feet are connected to your back through ligaments and muscles, so if you don't keep your back straight and strong, it will affect your footwork.

26. a. Stand in First Position,

    b. *demi-plié*, pressing both heels firmly into the floor,

    c. spring up, pushing strongly from the heels and drawing the toes slightly under the insteps so that you are in First Position on pointe, with the toes directly under the heels.

    d. Slide the toes outward as you lower the heels gently but firmly to the floor into a *demi-plié*, working through the *demi-pointe* and keeping the heels forward.

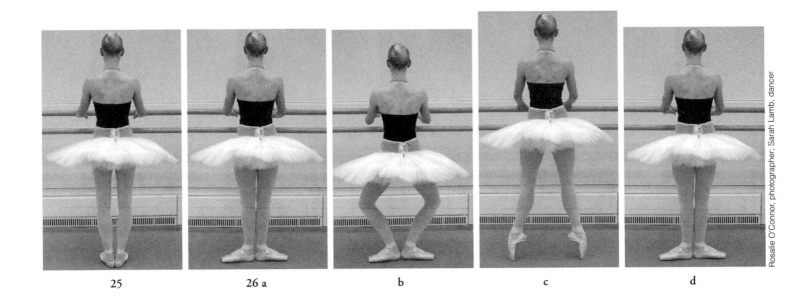

25   26 a   b   c   d

27. The same *relevé* in Second Position.

28. The same *relevé* in Open Fourth Position.

29. The same *relevé* in Crossed Fourth Position.

30. The same *relevé* in Fifth Position. Cross the feet so that they look like one foot. This is also called *soussus*, and may be taken in place or traveling to the front, back, or side.

27

28

29

30

DON'T DO THIS!

31. Don't lean on the barre. It takes the body out of its proper placement and balance.

32. Don't pull yourself up by pushing down on your arms. This is a good exercise for students of boxing, not ballet!

33. Don't push your stomach forward the achieve the position on pointe.

34. Don't let your heels twist back as you relevé.

35. Don't roll in on the arches or permit your knees to fall forward as you lower your heels.

36. Be sure to push the heels firmly into the floor each time you plié; don't let them pop up.

37. Don't let your back weaken.

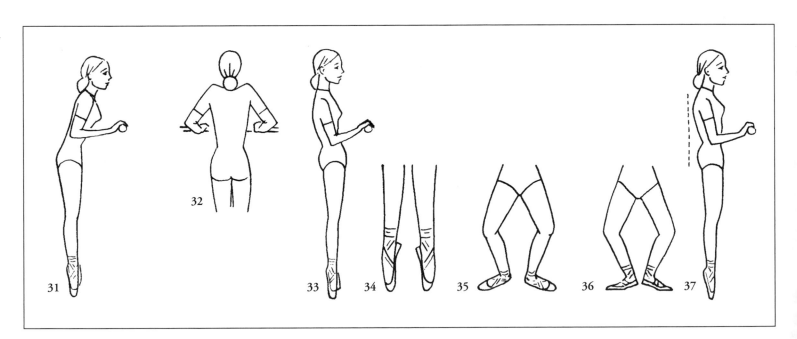

Échappé On Pointe

As in all of the steps described in this book the beginner should perform this step first at the barre, and later, when perfect control is gained, it may be practiced in the center without the aid of the barre.

Échappés may be performed in Second Position or Fourth Position. They may be taken *en face, en croisé, en éffacé,* or *en épaulé* and with or without changing of the feet in Fifth Position.

ÉCHAPPÉ À LA SECONDE WITHOUT CHANGE OF FEET

38. a. Ready to begin. Stand in Fifth Position with the right foot front, facing the barre and holding it with both hands, head erect, looking straight out,

    b. *demi-plié* in this position (heels down, knees back, body straight!). Count "And…"

    c. spring out to Second Position on pointe, pushing off strongly with the heels. (Pull up the knees, tighten the buttocks, lift up out of the hips, take a good, wide Second Position.) Count "One…"

    d. return the feet to Fifth Position, *fondu,* right foot front (both knees well opened out over the toes, back straight and strong). Count "And…" From this *plié* you are ready to perform the next *échappé.*

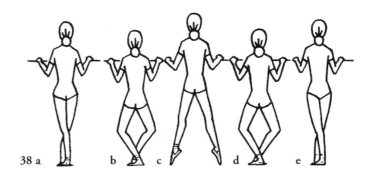

38 a   b   c   d   e

e. When you have finished a series of *échappés,* such as eight or sixteen, finish nicely by straightening the knees.

Repeat the *échappé* with the left foot front. The same *échappé* may also be performed changing the feet each time they close to Fifth Position, so that the right foot alternately closes back and front.

23

39 a   b   c   d   e   f

ÉCHAPPÉ EN CROISÉ AND ÉCHAPPÉ CHANGÉ

Here is an example of the *échappé* to Fourth Position, in this case performed *en croisé*, followed by an *échappé* changé to Second Position.

39. a. Ready to begin. Stand in Fifth Position with the right foot front, facing *en croisé*, arms in Fifth Position Low, head inclined to the right,

b. *demi-plié* in this position. Count "And…"

c. spring out to Fourth Position on pointe, at the same time raise the arms through Fifth Position Front to Third Position High with the left arm up, inclining the body slightly to the right. Count "One…"

d. return the feet to Fifth Position, *fondu*, with the right foot front, and at the same time lower the left arm, in front of the face, to Fourth Position Front. Count "And…"

e. spring out to Second Position on pointe, facing directly *en face*, and at the same time open the left arm to Second Position. Count "Two…"

f. close the feet to Fifth Position, *fondu*, with the left foot front, and at the same time turn the body to *croisé* and lower the arms to Fifth Position Low. Count "And." Repeat the entire step to the other side.

Don't Do This!

40. Don't keep the weight of the body over the back foot in Fourth Position; equalize the weight over both feet.

41. Don't permit the front leg to turn inward in the *échappé* in Fourth Position.

42. Don't mince the step by opening to a tiny Second Position.

43. Don't throw the feet so far apart that the position has no form.

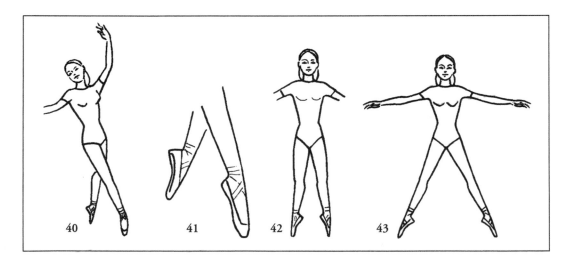

Relevé From Two Feet To One Foot

These relevés are sometimes called *relevé devant* and *relevé derrière*, sometimes *sissonne simple*. Terminology differs according to the Italian, French, and Russian schools. When the raised foot is transferred from the front to the back or from the back to the front, these *relevés* are called *relevé passé* or *sissonne passée la jambe*.

44. Stand in Fifth Position, right foot front, facing the barre and holding it with both hands. Have the body well centered, a good lift in the ribs, shoulders down, head erect, looking straight out.

RELEVÉ DEVANT

45. a. *Demi-plié*. Count "And…"

b. spring up onto the left pointe and at the same time raise the right foot to the *cou-de-pied devant* (or to the front of the left knee, in more advanced work). Count "One…"

c. close the right foot into Fifth Position, *fondu*, in front of the left foot. Count "And…"

44   45 a   b   c

46 a   b   c   47 a   b   c

RELEVÉ DERRIÈRE

46. a. *Demi-plié.* Count "And…"

   b. spring up onto the right pointe and at the same time raise the left foot to the *cou-de-pied derrière* (or behind the right knee, in more advanced work). Count "One…"

   c. close the left foot into Fifth Position, *fondu*, behind the right foot. Count "And."

RELEVÉ PASSÉ EN ARRIÈRE

47. a. *Demi-plié.* Count "And…"

   b. spring up onto the left pointe and at the same time raise the right foot to the front of the left knee. Count "One…"

   c. close the right foot into Fifth Position, *fondu*, behind the left foot. Count "And."

Relevé Passé En Avant

48. a. *Demi-plié.* Count "And..."

b. spring up onto the right pointe and at the same time raise the left foot to the back of the right knee. Count "One..."

c. close the left foot into Fifth Position, *fondu,* in front of the right foot. Count "And."

Repeat these *relevés* with the left foot front.

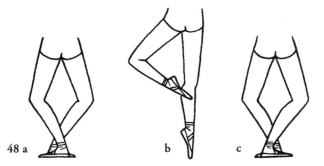

48 a   b   c

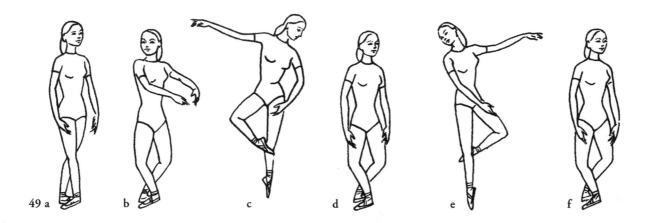

49 a   b   c   d   e   f

RELEVÉ DEVANT AND DERRIÈRE WITH AN EXAMPLE OF PORT DE BRAS AND BODY MOVEMENT

49. a. Ready to begin. Stand in Fifth Position, right foot front, facing *en croisé* (lower left corner of the room), arms in Fifth Position Low,

b. *demi-plié*. Count "And…"

c. spring up onto the left pointe, raising the right foot to the front of the left knee, incline the body and the head to the left and open the arms to Third Position Low, left arm front. Count "One…"

d. close the right foot into Fifth Position, *fondu*, in front of the left foot; at the same time straighten the body and return the arms to Fifth Position Low. Count "And…"

e. spring up onto the right pointe, raising the left foot to the back of the right knee, incline the body and the head to the right and open the arms to Third Position Low, right arm front. Count "Two…"

f. close the left foot into Fifth Position, *fondu*, behind the right foot; at the same time straighten the body and return the arms to Fifth Position Low. Count "And…"

Repeat this exercise several times with the right foot front, then repeat with the left foot front.

29

49 a   b   c   d   e   f

50 a   b   c   d

RELEVÉ PASSÉ EN ARRIÈRE WITH PORT DE BRAS

50. a. Ready to begin. Stand in Fifth Position, right foot front, facing *en face*, well centered, well lifted, arms in Fifth Position Low, head erect, looking straight out,

b. *demi-plié*, raise the arms to Fifth Position Front, incline the head to the left. Count "And..."

c. spring up onto the left pointe, raising the right foot to the front of the left knee, open the arms to Third Position High with the right arm up, incline the body and the head to the left and looking under the right arm. Count "One..."

d. close the right foot into Fifth Position, *fondu*, behind the left foot, open the arms outward and lower both of them to Fifth Position Low, inclining the head to the right. Count "And."

These *relevés* may be done in succession, alternating right foot and left foot. The arms must pass through Fifth Position Front each time before opening to Third Position High, in order to give form to their movement.

50 a   b   c   d

RELEVÉ PASSÉ EN AVANT WITH PORT DE BRAS

51. a. Ready to begin,

b. *demi-plié.* Count "And..."

c. spring up onto the right foot, raising the left foot to the back of the right knee; raise the arms to Fourth Position Front with the left arm across the body, incline the body to the left knee, turn the head to the left, and look at the left knee. Count "One..."

d. close the left foot into Fifth Position, *fondu,* in front of the right foot and open the left hand out toward the lower left corner of the room. Count "And..."

In performing these *relevés* in succession the arms do not pass through Fifth Position Front but merely open and close as they alternate. There are, of course, other *ports de bras* that may be used in the *relevés passés.* Those illustrated here are examples of such movement.

51 a   b   c   d

Glissade On Pointe

This step may be performed forward, backward, and sideward. It may be performed with a simple *dégagé* of the working foot or with a small *développé*. It may be done with or without changing the feet in closing to Fifth Position. The *glissade* illustrated here is with a change of feet.

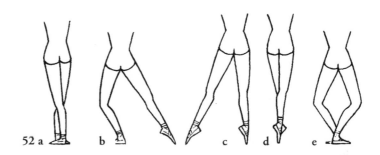

52 a   b   c   d   e

GLISSADE CHANGÉE

52. a. Ready to begin. Stand in Fifth Position, right foot front, facing the barre and holding it with both hands,

b. slide the right foot out to a strong point in Second Position with a very straight knee, at the same time bending the left knee in a good *demi-plié*. Count "And..."

c. step over onto the right pointe, taking the weight of the body over with you and pulling both knees up tight. Count "And..."

d. close the left foot, immediately, to Fifth Position on pointe, bringing it in front of the right and be sure to cross the feet well, pulling both knees up tight. Count "One..."

e. roll down the insteps, lowering both heels gently but firmly, into a *demi-plié* in Fifth Position. Count "And." If another *glissade* follows immediately, continue the "And" count into the sliding movement of the leg into Second Position.

GLISSADE CHANGÉE
(with small *Développé*)

53. a. Ready. Stand in Fifth Position, left foot front, *en face*, left shoulder slightly front, head turned slightly to the left, eyes looking to the lower left corner of the room, arms in Fifth Position Low

b. *demi-plié* on the right leg, raising the left foot to the *cou-de-pied devant*. Count "And..."

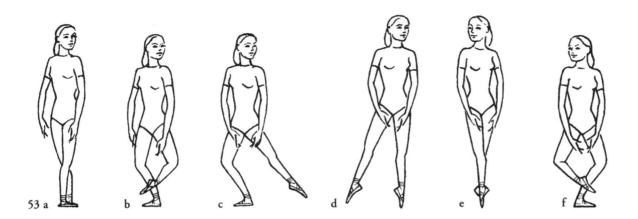

53 a   b   c   d   e   f

c. extend the left foot, straightening the knee in a low *développé*, (this is part of the above "And…" count)

d. step over onto the left pointe, taking the weight of the body with you and pulling the knees up tight. Count "A…"

e. close the right foot immediately to Fifth Position on pointe, in front of the left foot, bringing the right shoulder slightly forward and turning the head slightly to the right, look to the lower right corner of the room, cross the feet well, and pull both knees up tight. Count "One…"

f. roll down the instep of the left foot, gently lowering the heel to the floor in *fondu;* at the same time raise the right foot to the *cou-de-pied devant.* Count "And…"

Remember that the manner in which you come down from the full-pointe position to the *pied à terre*, or whole foot on the ground, is most important. You should always roll down through the *demi-pointe*, never jump from the full pointe to the flat. This is what makes all the difference between light, airy, soft movement and hard jerky movement.

Repeat the *glissade* with the left foot front. Repeat the *glissade* without changing the feet, both *derrière* and *devant.*

Piqué

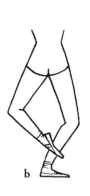

54 a   b   c   d

There are two ways of rising to a full-pointe position from the *pied à terre* position, where the whole foot rests on the floor.

One is the *relevé*, which has already been described, and the other is the *piqué*, or, as it is sometimes called, the *pose*. Again, the difference in terminology is that between the French and Italian schools. To *piqué* or *pose* means to step directly on to the full-pointe (or *demi-pointe*) position of the working foot and to raise the other foot into the air in any desired position such as *cou-de-pied, arabesque, attitude*, etc. *Piqués* may be performed to the front, to the back or to the side; they may be taken reaching out with the foot extended and the knee stretched, with or without a *développé*, or they may be taken close to the supporting foot, stepping with a bent knee and straightening it at the instant of stepping.

PIQUÉ EN ARRIÈRE, COUPÉ DESSUS

54.   a. Stand in Fifth Position, right foot front, facing the barre and holding it with both hands,

b. *demi-plié* on the right leg, raising the left foot to the lp *cou-de-pied derrière*. Count "And..."

c. step directly onto the full pointe of the left foot, just behind the right foot, straightening the left knee immediately as you step; at the same time raise the right foot to the *cou-de-pied devant* (or to the knee). Count "One..."

d. fall onto the right foot in a *coupé dessus* – that is, replace the left foot with the right, bending the knee in *fondu*, and at the same time raise the left foot to the *cou de pied derrière*. Count "And..."

55 a   b   c   d

Repeat the *piqué* with the left foot front.

The head plays an important part in all balletic movement. Here is the *piqué en arrière* and the *coupé dessus* performed with the movements of the head and arms:

55.   a. Ready to begin. Stand in Fifth Position, right foot front, *en face*, head erect, arms in Fifth Position Low,

b. *demi-plié* on the right leg and, as you raise the left foot to the *cou-de-pied derrière* position, incline the head to the right. Count "And…"

c. *piqué en arriére*, at the same time opening the arms to Third Position Low, with the right arm in front of the body, and incline the head to the left. Count "One…"

d. *coupé dessus*, fall onto the right foot directly over the left foot, at the same time moving the arms to the right into Third Position Low with the left arm in front, and incline the head to the right. Count "And…"

Take care that in the *coupé* you do not put the whole foot down flat but make the *fondu* movement of rolling down the instep as you *plié*.

Repeat the *piqué* with the left foot front.

The *piqué en arriére* may also be performed with an extended leg:

56. a. Ready. Stand in Fifth Position, right foot front, *en éffacé* (lower right corner of the room), arms in Fifth Position Low,

b. *demi-plié* on the right leg, extending the left to *éffacé derrière* and open the arms to the *demi-seconde* position. Count "And…"

c. step backward onto the full pointe of the left foot, stepping as far back as you can reach and taking the weight of the body with you as you step, at the same time raising the right foot to the front of the left knee and carrying the arms to Fourth Position Front. This may be done with either arm crossed over the body. If the right arm is crossed over, lean the body forward slightly over the right knee (illustrated); if the left arm is crossed over, lean the body and incline the head to the left. Count "One…"

d. *coupé dessus*, extending the left leg once again to *éffacé derrière*. Count "And."

Repeat the *piqué* with the left foot front.

56 a   b   c   d

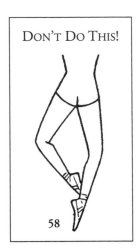

DON'T DO THIS!

57 a b c d 58

PIQUÉ EN AVANT, COUPÉ DESSOUS

57. a. Stand in Fifth Position, right foot front, facing the barre and holding it with both hands,

b. *demi-plié* on the left leg, raising the right foot to the *cou-de-pied devant*. Count "And…"

c. step directly onto the pointe of the right foot just in front of the left foot, at the same time raising the left foot to the *cou-de-pied derrière* (or in back of the knee). Count "One…"

d. *coupé dessous;* that is, fall onto the left foot, in *fondu,* under the right foot, and at the same time raising the right foot to the *cou-de-pied devant.* Count "And."

Repeat the *piqué* with the left foot front.

To perform the *piqué en avant* and *coupé dessous* in this manner with the head and arm movements, just reverse the action in Figure 55.

DON'T DO THIS!

58. Don't ever permit the supporting knee to be slack when standing on pointe. Always pull it up as tightly as possible. If the *piqué* is taken from a bent knee, straighten it at once as the weight is transferred. If the *piqué* is taken from an extended position, be sure that the knee is taut throughout.

The *piqué en avant* may also be taken with an extended leg:

59. a. Ready to begin. Stand in Fifth Position, left foot front, *en éffacé*, head erect, arms in Fifth Position Low,

b. *demi-plié* on the right leg and *dégagé* the left leg to *éffacé devant*, raising the arms to Fifth Position Front and inclining the body and head to the right. Count "And..."

c. *piqué en avant*, that is, step directly onto the left pointe taking the weight of the body with you, and immediately raise the right foot to the *cou-de-pied derrière* (or back of the

knee), at the same time raising the arms to Third Position high with the left arm high and look under the arm. Count "One..."

d. *coupé dessous*, that is fall on the right foot, in *fondu*, directly under the left foot, cutting the left out to *éffacé devant*. Count "And..."

Repeat the *piqué* with the right foot front.

This *piqué* may, of course, be performed with different *ports de bras*. It may also be performed *en croisé* or *en face*.

59 a   b   c   d

60 a   b   c   d

PIQUÉ EN ARABESQUE OUVERTE

60.   a. Ready to begin. Stand in Fifth Position, left foot front, *en éffacé* (lower left corner of the room), arms in Fifth Position Low, head inclined to right, looking out,

    b. *demi-plié* on the right leg, raise the left foot to the *cou-de-pied devant*. Count "And..."

    c. extend the left foot in a small *développé*, straightening the left knee, and raise the arms to Fifth Position Front. Count "A..."

    d. *piqué en avant* into *arabesque*, stepping out as far as the toe can reach and carrying the weight of the body over with you, at the same time opening the arms to *arabesque ouverte* (first arabesque) and straighten the head, looking out over the top of the left hand. Count "One..."

Repeat the *piqué en arabesque* with the right foot. Note carefully the difference between *piqué* and *relevé*.

60 a   b   c   d

Pas De Bourrée Piqué

When a *pas de bourrée* is said to be "*piqué*," this means that the movement is staccato or quick. As *piqué* means "pricked" or a pricking action, this literally means that the dancer pricks the floor with the sharp, quick, thrusting movements of the legs and feet.

This *pas de bourrée* may be taken *derrière, devant, dessous,* and *dessus.* The pas de bourrée dessous and dessus are often referred to as *pas de bourrée changé* because the feet change during the action of the step.

Described here is a *pas de bourrée changé – pas de bourrée piqué, dessous.*

61. a. Ready to begin. Stand in Fifth Position, right foot front, facing the barre and holding it with both hands,

b. *demi-plié* on the right leg, raising the left foot to the *cou-de-pied derrière.* Count "And…"

c. *piqué en arriére,* raising the right foot to the side of the left knee. Count "One…"

d. without coming off pointe on the left foot, *piqué* onto the right pointe, taking a step to the right side and raising the left foot to the side of the right knee. Count "And…"

e. without coming off pointe on the right foot, lower the left foot into Fifth Position on pointe in front of the right. Count "Two…"

f. *fondu* on the left leg; that is, roll down the instep through the *demi-pointe* into a good *demi-plié* with the left heel on the floor; at the same time raising the right foot to the *cou-de-pied derrière.* Count "And…"

The action of raising the knees as you *piqué* should be very sharp, and the piqué should be marked and strong.

Repeat the *pas de bourrée piqué* to the other side.

61 a   b   c   d   e   f

61 a   b   c   d   e   f

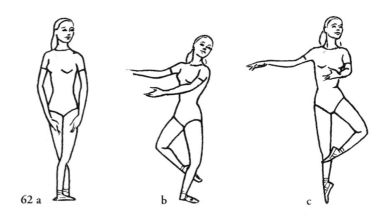

62 a   b   c

The *pas de bourrée* may be performed with many different *ports de bras*. Illustrated is a simple *port de bras* using the *épaulement*. Though the movements of the feet are sharp and staccato, the movements of the arms should not be jerky, but should flow.

62. a. Ready to begin. Stand in Fifth Position with the left foot front, *en face*, left shoulder slightly front, arms in Fifth Position Low, head erect and slightly turned to the left,

b. *demi-plié* on the left leg, at the same time raising the right foot to the *cou de pied derrière* and the arms to Fourth Position Front, bringing the left arm across the body and inclining the body to the left. Count "And…"

c. *piqué en arrière*, straightening the body and raising the left foot sharply to the side of the right knee. Count "One…"

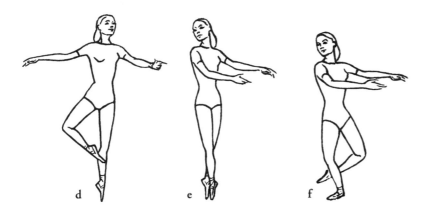

d. without coming off the right pointe, *piqué* onto the left pointe, taking a step to the left side and raising the right foot sharply to the side of the left knee; at the same time open the left arm out a little. Count "And…"

e. without coming off pointe on the left foot, close the right foot sharply into Fifth Position on pointe in front of the left, bringing the right shoulder front and the right arm across the body as the left opens to second, so that the arms are in Fourth Position Front with the right arm across, and

turn the head slightly to the right, holding it proudly erect. Count "Two…"

f. *fondu* on the right leg, raising the left foot to the *cou-de pied-derrière* and inclining the body to the right. Count "And…"

The shoulder position and the head position should be well defined each time the *pas de bourrée* is repeated.

Pas De Bourrée Couru, En Cinquième

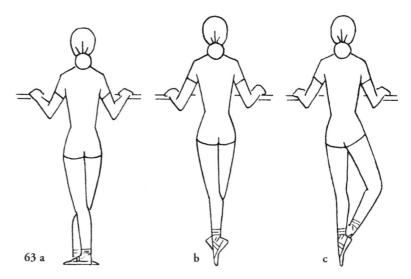

63 a   b   c

This is running *pas de bourrée* in Fifth Position, which may be performed traveling forward, backward, or sideward, or turning in place.

While it appears simple, this is actually a very difficult step to master, owing to the flexion of the knees and the necessity for taking very tiny steps at a very rapid speed to give the impression of skimming smoothly over the surface of the floor or stage.

Since the action of the knees is difficult to master, the proper study of this step begins at the barre, performing the *bourrées* in place, concentrating on the correct movement of the knees.

The following exercise, composed of tiny piqués, is a good preliminary exercise to establish the correct feeling for the knee action.

63. a. Ready to begin. Stand in Fifth Position, right foot front, facing the barre and holding it with both hands,

     b. *soussus,*

     c. bend the right knee slightly, raising it an inch off the floor. Count "And…"

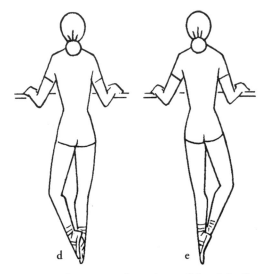

d   e

d. step on the pointe of the right foot in front and close to the left foot, simultaneously bending the left knee and raising the left foot an inch off the floor. As you step on the pointe of the foot, pull up tightly on the supporting knee until it is completely straight. Count "One..."

e. step on the pointe of the left foot behind and close to the right foot, simultaneously bending the right knee and raising the right foot an inch off the floor. As you step on the pointe, pull up tightly on the supporting knee until it

is completely straight. Count "Two..." Continue, in this manner, to take these tiny piqués, being careful to keep the legs well turned out from the hips, the heels forward, and the feet well crossed in Fifth Position each time the foot is placed down.

Repeat this exercise with the left foot front.

This flexing and straightening action of the knees is what makes the smooth floating effect of the *pas de bourrée couru*.

When the action of the knees is well understood and easily performed, the next stage in the study of this *pas de bourrée* may be undertaken. This is to *bourrée* rapidly in place, flexing and straightening the knees and vibrating the feet from the ankles without taking them off the floor.

In traveling, this action of the knees and feet must be preserved. Many students make the mistake of keeping their knees stiff in attempting the *bourrée*, others "sit" in the knees, giving them an ugly, bent appearance and the step a comical look.

The steps of the *pas de bourrée couru* MUST be tiny. The dancer travels by the speed of the feet rather than the size of the steps. The knees and feet must be kept close together at all times; in fact, the front foot is pushed along by the back foot. The legs must remain well turned out, the heels well forward and the feet well crossed so that at all times the back foot is seen as well as the front foot. The arms may be used in any given manner.

Examples of *port de bras* in *pas de bourrée couru*:

64. a. Stand on the right foot in a *demi-plié* with the left foot pointed to *croisé devant*, the body bent forward, head to the knee and inclined to the right, arms stretched forward and hands crossed at the wrists, left hand over right,

    b. *relevé*, drawing the extended foot into Fifth Position on pointe,

64 a   b   c   d   e   f   g

c. travel to the left side with tiny *bourrée* steps, passing the arms through Fifth Position front,

d. continue to travel to the left with tiny steps, flexing and straightening the knees, passing the arms to Third Position high with the left arm up,

e. continue to *bourrée* to the left and bring the right arm up to meet the left arm in Fifth Position high,

f. step to the left with the left foot (off pointe) and pass the right foot to the *cou de pied*,

g. take the right foot forward to *croisé devant*, sink into a good *demi-plié* on the left leg, at the same time bending the body forward, taking the head to the knee and inclining it to the left; stretch the arms forward, crossing the hands at the wrist with the right hand over the left.

Repeat the *pas de bourrée couru* to the other side.

64 a   b   c   d   e   f   g

Assemblé Soutenu, On Pointe

DESSUS

65. a. Ready to begin. Stand in Fifth Position, left foot front, facing the barre and holding it with both hands. Head erect, body well-centered and correctly placed,

b. slide the right foot out to a strong point in Second Position as the left leg bends in a good *demi-plié*. Count "And…"

c. spring into Fifth Position on pointe, pushing forcefully off the left heel and drawing the right foot into position in front of the left. Count "One…"

d. lower yourself gently to the *demi-plié*, passing through the *demi-pointes*.

Repeat this step with the right foot front.

To perform the *assemblé soutenu dessous*, reverse the action. Slide the front foot out to Second Position and close it behind in Fifth Position.

65 a   b   c   d

66 a   b   c   d   e

ASSEMBLÉ SOUTENU WITH AN EXAMPLE OF PORT DE BRAS

66. a. Ready to begin. Stand in Fifth Position, left foot front, *en face*, arms in Fifth Position Low, head erect,

b. as the right foot slides to Second Position, *fondu*, open the arms to *demi-seconde* position, inclining the body to the right and looking to the right foot. Count "And…"

c. on the spring into Fifth Position, right foot front, carry the right arm across the body to the left side and raise both arms, *à deux bras*, looking up to the top of the left hand, which is slightly higher than the right. Count "One…"

d. lower into Fifth Position, *fondu*, and continue to slide the left foot out to the pointe in Second Position, opening the arms to *demi-seconde* position, inclining the body to the left; look to the left foot. Count "And…"

e. spring again into Fifth Position on pointe, this time drawing the left foot into position in front of the right, carry the left arm across the body to the right side and raise both arms, *à deux bras*, looking up to the top of the right hand, which is slightly higher than the left. Count "Two…"

55

DESSOUS

67. a. Ready to begin. Stand in Fifth Position, left foot front, *en face*, arms in Fifth Position Low, head erect,

b. as the left foot slides out to Second Position, *fondu*, open the arms to *demi-seconde* position, incline the body to the right and the head to the right shoulder. Count "And…"

c. on the spring into Fifth Position on pointe, draw the left foot into position behind the right, carry the left arm across the body to the right, raising both arms *à deux bras*, look to the top of the right hand. Count "One…"

d. lower into Fifth Position, *fondu*, and continue to slide the right foot out to the point in Second Position, opening the arms to *demi-seconde* position and inclining the body to the left and the head to the left shoulder. Count "And…"

e. spring into Fifth Position on pointe, drawing the right foot into position behind the left; carry the right arm across the body to the left side, raising both arms *à deux bras*, and look to the top of the left hand. Count "Two…"

67 a   b   c   d   e

Coupé On Pointe, Fouetté Raccourci

68 a   b   c   d

68. a. Ready to begin. Stand in Fifth Position, right foot front, well centered, correctly placed, head erect, looking straight out, arms in Fifth Position Low,

b. *demi-plié* on the right leg, raising the left foot to the *cou-de-pied derrière* and the arms to Fifth Position Front, incline the head to the right. Count "And…"

c. *piqué en arriére* on the left pointe (page 38), throwing the right leg to Second Position en *l'air, à la demie-hauteur* (45° angle) and opening both arms to demi-seconde position, head erect. Count "One…"

d. lower into *demi-plié* on the left leg and at the same time whip the right foot behind the left leg, bending the right knee sharply without lowering the thigh, and bring the arms into Third Position Low, inclining the body and head to the left. Count "And…"

Repeat the *coupé* and *fouetté raccourci* with the other leg. The *port de bras* may also be taken with the arm in front corresponding to the raised leg and the body inclined to the raised knee at the finish of the *fouetté raccourci.*

68 a   b   c   d

Ballonné On Pointe

69. a. Stand in Fifth Position, right foot front, facing the barre, back straight, head erect,

b. *demi-plié* on the left leg and raise the right foot to the *cou-de-pied devant.* Count "And…"

c. spring up to a *relevé* on the left foot and throw the right foot out in a strong *développé* movement to Second Position *en l'air, à la demie-hauteur.* Do not raise the thigh; the movement takes place from the knee joint. Count "One…"

d. roll down the instep of the left foot into a *demi-plié* and bring the right foot back to the *cou-de-pied* position. Do not lower the thigh; the movement takes place from the knee joint. Count "And…"

Repeat this step several times on the same foot. Repeat it with the other foot. The working leg may also be closed in back of the ankle or it may alternate front and back.

70 a   b   c   d

Ballonné on pointe may be performed in the center, in either *écarté* or *éffacé* direction with the foot extending to Second Position or to Fourth Position, traveling diagonally across the stage. It is here illustrated *en éffacé*.

70. a. Ready to begin. Stand in Fifth Position, left foot front, *en éffacé* (lower left corner of room), arms in Fifth Position Low, head inclined to right, looking straight out,

b. *demi-plié* on the right leg, raising the left foot to the *cou-de-pied devant* and the arms to Fifth Position Front. Count "And...

c. spring up to a *relevé* on the right foot, traveling forward a little; throw the left foot out into a strong *développé* in Fourth Position *en l'air, à la demie-hauteur* and open the arms to Third Position High with the right arm high. Head is inclined to the raised arm. Count "One..."

d. roll down the instep of the right foot into a *demi-plié* and bring the left foot back to the *cou-de-pied* position. The arms remain in Third Position High. Travel a little forward on the *plié*. Count "And." Remember to keep the legs turned out from the hips, the heels forward, the back straight and strong and the working leg moving from the knee without raising and lowering the thigh.

These *ballonnés* may be performed in a series of 4, 8, 16, or 32 on the same foot.

Sissonne On Pointe

70 a   b   c   d

71 a b   c   d

Sissonnes may be taken on pointe in any desired pose and in various directions of the body. The *sissonne* may be opened with a *développé* or without. It may travel to the front, to the back, or to the side.

SISSONNE EN ARABESQUE

71. a. Ready to begin. Stand in Fifth Position, left foot front, *en croisé* (lower right corner of room), head inclined to the right, arms in Fifth Position Low,

b. *demi-plié.* Push the heels firmly into the floor. Count "And…"

c. spring up and out to *arabesque ouverte* (First Arabesque) on the left pointe, turning the body to face the left wall and traveling as much as possible. Count "One…"

d. close the right foot into Fifth Position, *fondu*, in front of the left foot, *en croisé* (lower left corner), head inclined to the left and arms lowered to Fifth Position Low. Count "And…"

Repeat the *sissonne* on the other foot.

Relevé On One Foot

This difficult step requires a great deal of strength in the back, the thighs, and the insteps. It is wise to practice these *relevés* diligently at the barre, not attempting to perform them in the center, until such time as the necessary strength can be commanded. *Relevés* on one foot may be performed in any given pose; they may be done in one place or traveling, facing in any of the body directions, or turning in place.

RELEVÉ EN ARABESQUE

72. a. Face the barre, holding it with both hands. Stand on the right foot, well turned out from the hip, with the left leg extended back in *arabesque à terre,* well turned out from the hip and with the foot correctly pointed on the edge of the big toe with the heel pressed down,

b. *demi-plié,* hold the back strong. Count "And…"

c. spring up into a *relevé* on the right foot, drawing the toes under the heel as you spring, pull the knees up tight, maintain the turnout of the legs. Do not pull on the barre. Count "One…"

d. lower, through the *demi-pointe,* into the *demi-plié* on the right leg. Maintain the strength of the back, do not permit the left leg to drop and keep a strong point in the left foot. Count "And…"

Repeat this *relevé* in a series of 4, 8, or 16 on the same foot. Repeat the series of *relevés* with the other foot

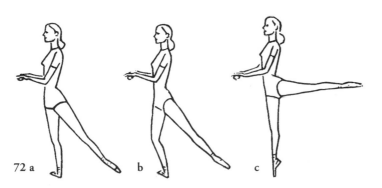

72 a   b   c   d

RELEVÉ EN ATTITUDE CROISÉ

73. a. Ready to begin. Stand in Fifth Position, right foot front, *en croisé* (lower left corner), arms in Fifth Position Low,

b. *demi-plié* and *chassé* forward to Fourth Position *Croisé*, taking the weight of the body forward over the front knee, which remains bent as the back knee straightens; raise the arms to Fifth Position Front and incline the head to the left. Count "And..."

c. spring up into a *relevé* in *attitude croisée* on the right pointe, pushing off both heels forcefully. Draw the toes under the body, arch the back, press the shoulders down and the left shoulder forward, inclining the head to the right and pulling the right knee up tight, raise the left knee, bending it sharply at a right angle, crossing the left leg well over in the back. Count "One..."

d. lower into a *demi-plié* on the right leg, maintaining the good *attitude* position. Don't forget to roll down the instep through the *demi-pointe*. Count "And..."

e. repeat the *relevé* in *attitude croisée* on count "Two."

Repeat this *relevé* in a series of 4, 8, or 16 on each foot.

73 a   b   c   d   e

Emboîté On Pointe

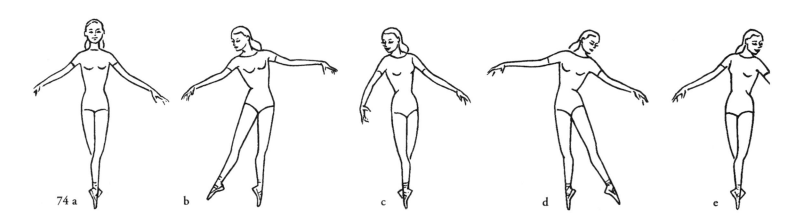

74 a   b   c   d   e

This step is quite different from the *emboîté* that is *sauté*. *Emboîté* on pointe is a series of walking steps on the pointes performed in Fifth Position.

74. a. Ready to begin. Stand in Fifth Position, left foot front, *en face*, arms in *demi-seconde*. *Demi-plié* and *soussus*,

b. keeping both knees pulled up tightly, *dégagé* the right foot to a small Second Position, bend forward slightly and look toward the right foot. Count "And..."

c. close the right foot into Fifth Position, on pointe, in front of the left foot. Count "One..."

d. *dégagé* the left foot to a small Second Position, looking toward the left foot. Count "And..."

e. close the left foot into Fifth Position, on pointe, in front of the right foot. Count "Two."

Continue to walk in this manner, advancing toward the front of the room, and crossing the feet well each time in Fifth Position. Keep the insteps well pulled up at all times.

When the action is reversed and the feet close behind in Fifth Position each time, so that the dancer recedes from the front of the stage to the back, this step is called "*déboîté.*"

65

74 a   b   c   d   e

Demi-Plié, On Pointe

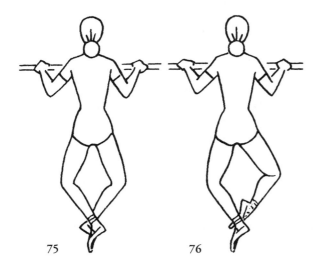

75

76

In taking the *demi-plié* on pointe the dancer must hold the ankle very strongly. The arch does not force over – on the contrary, the instep and ankle are tense and the heel is held firmly. Beginners will find this very difficult to do and should approach the study of this movement slowly and carefully, practicing it first on two feet in all the positions and later on one foot, when the instep is sufficiently strong to hold under this pressure

75. *Demi-plié* in Fifth Position.

76. *Demi-plié* on one foot.

This *demi-plié* may be practiced at the barre in many ways. An example is the *jeté piqué*.

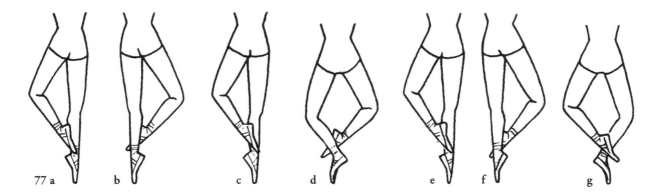

77 a   b   c   d   e   f   g

77.   a. From Fifth Position with the right foot front, facing the barre and holding it with both hands, *demi-plié* and execute a *relevé derrière* (page 23).   Count "And..."

b. *jeté piqué* onto the left foot.   That is, without coming down off pointe, step onto the left foot directly under the right and raise the right foot to the *cou-de-pied devant*.   Pull the left knee up tight and press the right knee well open.   Count "One..."

c. *jeté piqué* onto the right foot.   That is, without coming down off pointe, step onto the right foot directly over the left and raise the left foot to the *cou-de-pied derrière*.   Pull the right knee up tight and press the left knee well open.   Count "And..."

d. *jeté piqué en fondu* onto the left foot.   That is, bend the left knee in a *demi-plié* as you step on the left point.   Press both knees well open.   Count "Two, and..."

e. *jeté piqué* onto the right foot.   Count "One..."

f. *jeté piqué* onto the left foot.   Count "And..."

g. *jeté piqué en fondu* onto the right foot, inclining the head to the right.   Count "Two, and..."

Continue to repeat this set of steps several times on the same side.   Then repeat on the other side.

When the insteps are strong enough, this same exercise may be performed in the center without the aid of the barre.

68

Sauté On Pointe

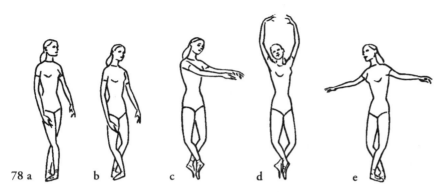

78 a   b   c   d   e

Jumps on pointe are among the most difficult technical feats to perform. They should not be undertaken until the full strength of the feet, legs, and back has been developed. Much practice on the *demi-pliés* on pointe should precede the study of jumps on pointe. When you are able to hold the ankles and heels strongly in the *demi-pliés*, you are ready to begin the study of jumps on pointe.

Jumping on pointe may be performed on two feet, on one foot, or from foot to foot.

SAUTÉ ON POINTE AND CHANGEMENT

78.   a. Ready to begin. Stand in Fifth Position, right foot front, *en croisé* (lower left corner), arms in Fifth Position Low,

     b. *demi-plié*, inclining the head to the left. Count "And…"

c. jump up onto the pointes in Fifth Position, right foot front, raise the arms to Fifth Position Front; the head remains inclined to the left. Count "One…"

d. jump again onto the pointes without changing the feet and raise the arms to Fifth Position high, looking under the arms. Count "And…"

e. *changement*, off pointe, finishing in a *demi-plié* in Fifth Position with the left foot front. As you jump, turn the body to face the lower right corner, so that you are again *en croisé*, and open the arms outward to Second Position with the palms open, inclining the body and the head to the right. Count "Two, and…"

Repeat the entire step on the other side.

PAS DE CHEVAL

79. a. Ready to begin. Stand in Fourth Position on pointe, *en éffacé* (lower left corner), with the left foot pointed front, the right knee bent in a *demi-plié*, arms in *demi-seconde*, body bent slightly forward, looking toward the left foot,

b. spring lightly upward off the right pointe and raise the left foot to the right knee. Count "And…"

c. alight on the pointe of the left foot in *demi-plié* and raise the right foot to the left knee. Count "A…"

d. without stopping the action of the right leg continue to develop it to Fourth Position *à la demie-hauteur*. (This is part of the same count as c. above).

e. Continue the movement of the right foot until it points out on the floor. Count "One."

Repeat the step with the other foot. Continue to repeat the step, alternating the feet and traveling diagonally downstage.

79 a   b   c   d   e

SAUTILLÉ ON POINTE

Little hops on the pointe of one foot are often the highlight of the variations from the classical repertoire. They may be performed in any given pose and also changing from one pose to another. For example, the dancer may begin with a *relevé* in *attitude devant*. From this position she will hop lightly and rapidly on the supporting pointe, carrying the raised leg slowly around from *attitude devant* to *attitude éffacée*, traveling backward the entire time. When she has reached the *attitude éffacé* and the end of the sequence of hops, she will sharply straighten both knees into a pose in *éffacé derrière*, holding the balance on pointe as long as possible before closing the feet to Fifth Position off pointe.

11
A Look at the
USA International Ballet Competition

Janice Barringer

The first City of Jackson Grand Prix winners Nina Ananiashvili and Andris Liepa (both USSR) at the 1986 USA IBC.

Introduction to Part II
How does a Dancer Prepare to Enter an International Ballet Competition?

If you find that you love ballet after going beyond the beginner and lower intermediate level, consider entering a ballet competition in the future. Although it is not imperative for a dancer to win or even enter a dance competition, there is no doubt that it can be beneficial to a career. If this is something that you aspire to, you must expect a period of intense preparation.

First, you must know what your aspirations are: do you love dance and want to pursue it as a hobby or as an actual career? Do you see yourself using ballet as technical support to jazz, tap or other forms of dance? A well-trained pointe dancer definitely has the edge over people who have not had this experience just from the sheer strength that is developed during the training. Or do you really have dreams of joining a classical ballet company and have it as your sole means of support?

If the latter is what you are seeking, then entering a ballet competition might be desirable for several reasons. It will definitely improve your technique because of the added hours and months of rehearsal necessary to prepare. Invaluable experience will be gained not only from the months of preparation, but also from the competition itself, exposing you to different styles, choreography and opinions. You will be broadened by improved technique, style, and a greater knowledge of the dance world, and, it might possibly jump-start your career by the exposure. There are always company directors, teachers, and coaches who are looking for extraordinary dancers, or extraordinary potential.

At what level of development is a dancer ready to consider competing? A student can quite quickly learn the basic steps in ballet, placement, positions and aplomb. But simply being proficient in execution is not enough to expect to be up to the demands of what is expected from a dancer in a ballet competition. The competitor should have exceptional technique and an artistic sensibility as well as drive, determination and a love of ballet. The choreography choices to be performed require the dancer, no matter how young, to be on an advanced level. After all, competitions are the equivalent of the Olympic Games for dancers!

The first step is to find a good school staffed by professionals. The teachers in such schools have strong backgrounds. They have probably danced professionally in ballet companies, though not necessarily, and have impressive teaching qualifications. The curriculum and policies are set from an extensive knowledge of ballet and an understanding of the importance of adhering to strict standards.

Once you have found a school that emphasizes the serious study of ballet, it is time for you to make a commitment. A commitment of time, energy and money is essential if you expect to develop the advanced technique required for a professional career. The expense is greater for girls because they must work a good deal of the time in pointe shoes.

Finding an experienced and willing coach is also essential. Simply taking class with a good teacher is not enough. Rehearsal and coaching outside the classroom is where the real work for a competition must occur. A student cannot possibly prepare himself or herself to compete. Advice from a good coach concerning choice of choreography, music, costumes, and refining technique and style must be carefully directed and guided by a dedicated mentor.

If a company cannot or will not loan or rent costumes and music, the dancer must provide for these himself/herself. While it is not necessary to dance with a partner, most people entering ballet competitions prefer to dance *pas de deux* rather than solos. The partner may or may not be a competitor. (In some competitions, all participants must compete.) All of these considerations should be carefully taken into account when planning and budgeting time and money.

To succeed in dance to the point of being chosen to compete in these prestigious international competitions, individuals must be self-disciplined and completely driven. No one else can live this dream for them. They must have no doubts that this is the path to be followed.

The Differences between Competitions

When reading the many magazines devoted to dance, one is aware of the existence of a number of dance competitions. The advertisements feature dancers of all ages in flashy costumes, winning awards and titles. There are even entire sections covering these competitions with appropriate information if one is interested in participating in them.

While they are extremely popular and successful, it is important to distinguish between this type of dance competition and those focused primarily on classically-trained dancers, such as the USA International Ballet Competition in Jackson, Mississippi, the IBC in Varna, Bulgaria, the IBC in Moscow, Russia, the IBC in Helsinki, Finland, the Prix de Lausanne, Switzerland and the New York International Ballet Competition (established in 1984).

If a dancer is primarily interested in a career in ballet, the information in Part II about the USA IBC will be invaluable. While the other type of competition is good experience for preparing to enter the competitive world of dance, it has less value for a dancer who wants acceptance into a ballet company. It is important to be thoroughly versed in the differences between the two.

Janie Parker, Senior gold medalist, and William Pizzuto, Senior silver medalist (both of the USA) at the 1982 USA IBC. (Together, Parker and Pizzuto were Senior best couple winners.)

One way to tell the difference between the two types of dance competitions is the professional affiliations of the judges: the jury in ballet competitions consists of either prominent former ballet dancers, former or current directors of ballet companies around the world, or teachers from leading international ballet schools. While some dance school competitions may have notable ballet judges, most of them have backgrounds in musical theater or show business.

Another way in distinguishing between the two types is the categories in which one must compete. In international ballet competitions there are lists of variations or *pas de deux* from which the competitors must choose to perform. These are always from well-known classical ballets. In order to enter, hopeful competitors typically must send a video to be screened by eminent people in the ballet world. A few are chosen to compete; many are not. Competitions consist of (typically) three rounds, in which dancers must perform not only the required classical works, but also one or two contemporary pieces of choreography. Tap, hip hop or street dancing are never included. After each round, some dancers are eliminated by the jury

Any time there is confusion in sorting this out, call the nearest professional ballet company for advice and direction.

Kathy Thibodeaux (USA), Senior silver medalist, at the 1982 USA IBC.

International Ballet Competitions

The number of international ballet competitions has steadily increased since the 1960s—which makes it impossible to list them all here. A certain few are presented under the auspices of the International Dance Committee of the International Theatre Institute (ITI) and are sanctioned by the Conseil International de la Dance (CID) of UNESCO (an arm of the United Nations). The ones that fall into this category are Varna, Moscow, Helsinki, Jackson and New York. As in the USA IBC in Jackson, all listed below are open to students and professionals except for Youth American Grand Prix which is only for students.

- *IBC in Varna, Bulgaria*
  The first IBC in the world was held in 1964 in this resort town on the shores of the Black Sea. It is a biennial event. One unusual aspect of this event is that all performances are presented on the stage of an open-air theater. In 2004 there were 129 entries from 29 countries. Forty-two competitors from sixteen countries were admitted to the second round, and in the final, or third, round, twenty-two dancers from twelve countries participated. The website is www.bulgarianspace.com/music/varna_ibc.

- *IBC in Moscow, Russia*
  The Moscow Competition was established in 1969. Like Jackson, it is held every four years. Because ballet is highly regarded in Russian culture, the local public which attends the performances is one of the most enthusiastic and knowledgeable in the world. In 1993, for organizational and economic reasons, it lost the official sanction of CID and UNESCO, but regained this status in 2004. The website is: www.russianballet.ru/competition/eng.

- *IBC in Helsinki, Finland*
  The quadrennial Helsinki Competition, established in 1984, attracts many European and Russian competitors. Held in Finland's capital city, its aspects are very similar to the Jackson competition. The website is www.balcomphel.fi. The email address for the competition secretary is ballet@balcomphel.fi.

- *The New York IBC*
  Established in 1984 and held every three years in New York City, this competition has a unique format: the repertory to be performed is not announced until the competitors' arrival in New York. Prior to this time the dancers do not know what dances they were to perform.

All dancers are taught three *pas de deux* by esteemed teachers and coaches in the first two weeks. The judges find it easier to compare the dancers when they are dancing the same works. A contemporary solo of the competitor's choice is required also. During the third week the four performances of the competition as well as the closing gala take place in Lincoln Center. The website is www.nyi.org.

OTHER MAJOR COMPETITIONS

◆ *Prix de Lausanne*
Established in 1973 and backed by Rosella Hightower and Maurice Bejart, it is a week-long competition for young dancers of all nationalities, aged fifteen to seventeen, who want to pursue a professional career but are not yet professionals. About 120 candidates from thirty countries compete each year, in the hope of being selected for the finals of the competition, reserved for the best fifteen among them. Candidates are not judged on the basis of just one or two performances, but on their dancing in classic and contemporary dance classes throughout the week of the competition. The Prix de Lausanne awards scholarships and apprentice scholarships with international ballet companies; it does not award cash prizes. Its website is www.prixdelausanne.org.

◆ *Youth American Grand Prix*
A student ballet competition in America that awards scholarships to the leading dance schools in the U.S. and abroad. The competition is held annually in New York and is open to dance students of all nationalities nine to nineteen years old. Launched in 2000 by two former dancers of the Bolshoi Ballet, it was created to provide educational and professional opportunities for young dancers. The website is www.yagp.org.

◆ *The American Ballet Competition*
New on the scene, this competition was first held in June, 2004 in Miami, Florida, under the auspices of New World School of the Arts / Dance Division and continues to be held yearly in Miami. This competition is open only to students who hope to go on to a professional career in ballet. Those eligible to compete are Juniors (ages eleven and twelve), Seniors (ages thirteen to fifteen) who compete for cash prizes and scholarships offered by prestigious dance schools and companies. A Pre-professional Division (ages sixteen to nineteen) has been added to accommodate several professional American companies that are offering traineeships as prizes. Its website is www.americanballetcompetition.com.

Jennifer Gelfand and Edward Stierle (both USA),
both Junior gold medalists, at the 1986 USA IBC

Katia Carranza (Mexico) and Mikhail Ilyin (USSR),
both Senior bronze medalists, at the 2002 USA IBC

What is the USA International Ballet Competition?

Every four years, for two weeks at the end of June and overlapping into July, dancers from around the world come to Jackson, Mississippi, to compete for prizes and study with master teachers. This Olympics-style competition has talented, well-trained young dancers vying for gold, silver and bronze medals, cash awards, scholarships and jobs.

At the conclusion of the first competition, a sanction was received from the International Dance Committee of the International Theater Institute of UNESCO for the USA IBC, a distinction it still holds today. In this way, Jackson joined other ITI-sanctioned competitions that rotated each year among the most prestigious of competitions. A Joint Resolution of Congress designated the Jackson competition as the United States' official international ballet competition in 1982. On July 10, 2004, the USA IBC celebrated its twenty-fifth anniversary with a Reunion Gala at Thalia Mara Hall in Jackson.

History of the USA International Ballet Competition

AN IDEA IS CONCEIVED

The first great international ballet competition, held in 1964 in the seaside resort of Varna, Bulgaria, has been of seminal importance. The regulations set in Varna have been adopted, with certain exceptions, by many of the other major competitions that followed.

> Some of the now legendary dancers who became known for the first
> time in Varna are Vladimir Vassiliev ('64), Ekaterina Maximova ('65),
> Natalia Makarova ('65), Mikhail Baryshnikov ('66), Eva Evdokimova ('70),
> Fernando Bujones ('74), Yoko Morishita ('74), Evelyn Hart ('80),
> Vladimir Malakhov ('86), Elizabeth Platel ('78) and Sylvie Guillem ('83).

In 1974 Randolph Swartz, a dance presenter in Philadelphia, saw, on television, a beautiful performance of *The Dying Swan* by the famous Russian ice skating team Oleg and Ludmila Protopopov. They had won the gold medal in both the 1964 and 1968 Winter Games of the Olympics. Always looking for new ballet audiences, Randy thought perhaps a ballet competition in the United States would be a good idea. He immediately called

Vadim Pisarev (USSR), Senior gold medalist, at the 1986 USA IBC.

© Hubert Worley

84

William Como, Editor in Chief of *Dance Magazine*, and presented his idea of a competition in the hope that it could be televised and thus generate a wider interest in the art.

Mr. Como said that he and several other people in New York were already entertaining the idea of a dance competition in the United States. He invited Randy to join them at their next meeting. When he arrived at the offices of *Dance Magazine* in New York, he joined a gathering of some of the most prestigious and accomplished people in the world of dance. Among those luminaries were Walter Terry, noted dance critic for the *Saturday Review*, an author of numerous books and a former dance critic for the *New York Herald Tribune*; Donald Saddler, internationally-known choreographer and director; Natasha Deakin, program director of the Institute of International Education; Genevieve Oswald, Curator of the Dance Collection at the New York Public Library for the Performing Arts at Lincoln Center; Jane Hermann, Director of Special Events at the Metropolitan Opera Association at Lincoln Center; and Mr. Como. The outcome of this meeting in the spring of 1974 was the decision to incorporate what was to become the International Ballet Competition.

Jackson is Chosen

After a full life and career around the world and in New York,

Thalia Mara, dance educator, performer and author, moved in 1975 to Jackson, Mississippi. She had been hired to develop the Jackson Ballet, as Artistic Director, of the first professional ballet company in the state. Her intention was to bring the company to national recognition. Within the very first year, Thalia recognized that her dream would never be realized without first creating a ballet audience. Ballet performances at the 2400-seat Municipal Auditorium (now named Thalia Mara Hall) were drawing audiences of only 200 to 300 people. It was obvious to her that football was the big draw in Mississippi, not dance.

Always thinking big, Thalia realized that if she could bring the International Ballet Competition to Mississippi, it might create some interest with Mississippians because of the athleticism of the dancers and the awarding of medals as in the Olympic Games. Thalia approached Cliff Finch, the newly-elected governor, with her idea, and persuaded him to call a meeting of prominent business people in the community. Fortunately, at about that time, the city of Jackson was looking for an event that would bring tourism, business and notice to the city and state. To Thalia, it was a perfect fit.

In 1978 Jacksonians formed a nonprofit corporation called Mississippi Ballet International Inc. to produce the competition. It was responsible for all of the local logistics such as housing, public relations, marketing, and fundraising. So it came about that the IBC Inc., Mississippi Ballet International Inc., and the citizens of Mississippi joined forces to bring about this extraordinary event. An idea that was sparked in the minds of those very accomplished people in New York now was being ignited by a very ambitious, efficient, energetic and personable group lead by Thalia Mara.

It had taken four years of meeting and planning to bring the original idea to fruition. When the first competition was held in June of 1979, seventy dancers from fifteen countries participated.

Donald Saddler suggested an opening ceremony similar to the Olympics: accompanied by a symphony orchestra, the competitors would march down the aisles of the auditorium following the flag of their country. As the dancer's name was announced, he or she would be presented with a rose and move

The Honorary Founders Committee was comprised of Thalia Mara, William Como, Dale Danks Jr., Natasha Deakin, Dr. Richard Freis, Tom Hederman, Jane Hermann, Herman Hines, Claudia Hogg, Robert Joffrey, Donald Lutken, Genevieve Oswald, Donald Saddler, Tom Scott Jr., Rosalind Welch Seabrook, Albert Simmons, Jean (Sister) Simmons, Cecil Smith, Estelle Sommers, Harry Strauss, Walter Terry, and Martha Underwood.

© Hubert Worley

Picture: Irina Dvorovenko (USSR), Junior silver medalist at the 1990 USA IBC .

to a choreographed position on stage. A similar version of the opening ceremony continues today.

When the 1979 USA IBC ended, the IBC Inc. dissolved, turning the project over to Mississippi Ballet International Inc. Later the name was changed to what it is today, the USA International Ballet Competition.

It was important to the Americans to have Russian involvement in the competition from the very first, because of their long tradition of producing remarkable dancers and teachers. Their presence would bring prestige to this new American competition. The first representative was the long-time Director of the Bolshoi Academy, Sophia Golovkina. She and Robert Joffrey co-chaired the first jury. When Golovkina returned to Russia, she reported to Yuri Grigorovich, Director of the Bolshoi, that this new competition on American soil was fair, well-organized and had reached a remarkable professional level of artistry.

By the time of the second competition in 1982, the political situation between the United States and the Soviet Union had deteriorated because of the war in Afghanistan. All cultural exchanges between the two countries had come to a standstill.

Robert Joffrey, an international diplomat for dance, was a key player in negotiating the participation of Russian dancers in the 1986 competition. Like Thalia, he thought that ballet united the world. His efforts paid off: the Russians came in force in 1986. Yuri Grigorovich, Artistic Director of the Bolshoi Ballet, was named co-chairman of the jury along with Mr. Joffrey. By 1994, some of the dancers who came from the newly created republics, like Kazakhstan and the Baltic, were outstanding. They were successful at the competition and were offered contracts with ballet companies world-wide. There is no question that Jackson has been a bridge between the formerly separate dance worlds.

Thalia Mara and Yuri Grigorovich, Director of the Bolshoi Ballet and Co-chairman of the International Jury, at Opening Night of the 1986 USA IBC.

DISTINGUISHED PARTICIPANTS

From the very beginning, legendary names in the ballet world have been associated with the Jackson Competition. Experts in this field and in others have contributed their experience, knowledge and the drawing power of their names to make this competition special. Besides the distinguished jury and dance school faculty, the Master and Mistress of Ceremonies have included such dance legends as Alexandra Danilova, Magda Saleh, Marcos Paredes, Oleg Briansky, Carmen de Lavallade, Ivan Nagy, Magdalena Popa, Dennis Nahat, Ann Reinking, Alexander Grant, Janie Parker, Robert Barnett and Anna-Marie Holmes.

AN ANGEL APPEARS

William D. Mounger.

William D. Mounger (better known as Billy) joined the board of directors as its chairman in 1994 and has been chairman ever since. As a succesful businessman, he realized that the competition was good for Jackson and Mississippi, and has essentially raised most of the funds necessary for its operations. A foundation has been established to ensure that this prestigious competition continues.

In 1994 Hillary Rodham Clinton was honorary chair of the competition. Honorary directors over the years have been Gene Kelly in 1990, Cynthia Gregory in 1998 and Edward Villella in 2002. In 1982 a local resident, the renowned author Eudora Welty, was an honored guest along with Ben Sommers, president of Capezio Ballet Makers, Inc.

How the Competition is Organized

THE STAFF

The competition staff is headed by the Executive Director who develops, directs, and oversees the USA IBC budget, directs operations, supervises office staff, determines volunteer committee needs and represents the USA IBC board of directors at sanctioned competitions and international dance meetings around the world. The Executive Director is the official spokesperson of the organization.

The General Manager serves as the business manager for the competition and is responsible for office facilities and finances. In addition, he/she manages the online store and general sales for IBC commemorative merchandise.

The Artistic Administrator is responsible for competitor relations as well as many artistic aspects of the IBC. He/she also manages the CityDance program and the IBC Summer Arts Camp.

The Director of Public Relations is responsible for media relations, marketing, advertising, and the IBC newsletter.

The Box Office Manager rounds out the competition staff.

THE COMPETITION PROGRAM

The competition consists of three rounds. In the first (elimination) round, competitors must perform either two solo variations or one *pas de deux* selected from a specific list of classical ballet repertoire compiled by officials. The lists are different for the junior division (ages 15 to 18) and senior division (ages 19 to 26). Total stage time is limited to three minutes for each variation or twelve minutes for *pas de deux*. If the competitors score seven points (in a ten point system), they may continue to round two. A feature of the competition of which officials are very proud is that even when dancers are eliminated, they may stay to the end of the entire competition as observers. Their expenses will continue to be paid by the USA IBC.

> While the first competition in Jackson was in 1979 and the second was in 1982, the rest have been held every four years—1986, 1990, 1994, 1998 and 2002. The length of the competition is about two weeks. In the summer of 2004 a Gala Performance was held at Thalia Mara Hall in Jackson to commemorate the 25th Anniversary of the USA IBC.

Unlike the Varna and Moscow competitions, Jackson limits the second (semifinal) round exclusively to contemporary choreography. The USA IBC is interested in dances for this round by such choreographers as George Balanchine, Twyla Tharp, Jiri Kilian, Hans Van Manen, Ben Stevenson, William Forsythe, Jerome Robbins, Eliot Feld, and Paul Taylor. The semifinalists must perform one contemporary solo or duet, and total stage time must not exceed six minutes. To progress to round three (the final round), competitors must receive seven points in a ten-point system.

In round three, finalists must perform a *pas de deux* or two solo variations of their choice from the required classical ballet repertoire set by the IBC. Juniors and seniors choose from the same repertory. In addition, they must also perform a contemporary solo or duet. As in the first round, total stage time must not exceed three minutes for each variation or twelve minutes for *pas de deux*.

Contemporary works from the second and third rounds are eligible for a choreography award. Original choreography created especially for the competition is also eligible for this award.

© Hubert Worley

Lauren Gelfand, Junior bronze medalist, and Daniel Meja (both USA) at the 1990 USA IBC.

How the Jury Judges a Competitor

The jury evaluates and judges the performances of the participating dancers. Artistry, musicality, line, taste, technique, stylistic knowledge and charisma or individual personality are what the judges are looking for. The expressiveness of the dancer is encouraged. While technique is important, it is merely a means to express artistry. (The judges take into account that there are aspects the young dancer can't control, such as the taste of the people who have been working with them.) They tend to ignore the peripheral: whether or not the dancers wear expensive, professional costumes, if their recordings are scratchy, or if they fall. The judges want the dancers to really dance...to breathe...to make technique invisible; real dancing, not just required steps.

At the time this book was written, the jury consisted of thirteen people from all over the world who are experienced, knowledgeable and respected in dance. For fairness, there are never two judges from the same country.

At the first competition, Robert Joffrey, founder of the Joffrey Ballet, shared the Jury Chairmanship with Sophia Golovkina of the USSR, director of the Bolshoi Ballet School. Joffrey was the sole chairman in 1982, but shared it again in 1986 with Yuri Grigorovich of the USSR, Director of the Bolshoi Ballet. The 1990 competition was dedicated to the memory of Mr. Joffrey, who died on March 25, 1988.

Boston Ballet Artistic Director Bruce Marks took over the job of chairman of the jury in 1990. The role of chairman is to help set the rules, choose the required repertory and guide the jury in understanding its task. He also chooses jury members with the goal of finding people who have broad dance backgrounds.

The scoring is based on a number system from one to ten with one being the lowest, and ten, the highest. The jury includes scores from all competitive rounds in the final score. As Bruce says, "sometimes dancers make the wrong choices. They might choose their best piece to dance in the first round. We don't want to penalize them for not knowing which piece is their best. Therefore, we include all the scores to get a final score." To avoid the appearance of a juror acting in a partisan manner, the system eliminates the top and bottom numbers. Thalia Mara set the tone early on with the jury. Even though she wasn't a member, she stood over the jurors like a mother hen. She made it clear that they were to keep very high standards. Artistry was to be valued over acrobatics and tricks.

The jury chairman feels it is most important that the competition be perceived as fair and as having high artistic standards. In his second competition as chairman (1994) Marks coined the phrase "the process is the prize." In other words, the real prize is not winning a medal but going through the entire experience. He says, "Just the time spent preparing for the competition with your coach should be one of great growth. Once you get here, seeing other young dancers, watching how they work, gaining friendships and being seen is all very valuable and life-changing."

Another component that Marks has instigated is giving the competitors feedback on their performances. Jurors are required to make comments on their scoring sheets in the event dancers would like to discuss their strengths and weaknesses.

Vladimir Malakhov (USSR), Senior bronze medalist, at the 1990 USA IBC.

Requirements for Entry

1. The ages of competitors must fall into two groups: Juniors, 15 to 18 years, and Seniors from 19 to 26 years.

2. Competitors may appear either as soloists or as couples.

3. Couples may be formed between members of the same division or separate age divisions.

4. Auditions: anyone interested in participating in the USA IBC must submit a video with music. The film should be shot straight-on with the full body in view. The applicant must wear practice clothes in a color that is in contrast to the background. Videos of live performances will not be accepted. A committee of three meets in Jackson and screens the audition films for a period of two weeks. It takes into consideration where the dancer is working, with whom he or she is working, the level of the dancing, and finally, the quality of the dancing. Detailed information about all aspects of the competition can be accessed on the website: www.usaibc.com

5. Choreography: A list of approved choreographic choices can be found on the USA IBC website. Competitors are restricted to the choreography found on this list.

6. Music: Competitors must furnish their own musical material which must be on CDs, reel-to-reel tapes or mini discs. Two recordings for each selection are required for performances and another for rehearsals. If the dancer prefers piano accompaniment, he or she must bring a pianist at his or her own expense or request on the application form that one be provided by the competition free of charge. Sheet music must be brought by the competitor for the works to be performed.

Johan Kobborg, Grand Prix winner, and Henrietta Muus (both Denmark) at the 1994 USA IBC.

Awards, Housing, Hospitality and Host Families

AWARDS

If a competitor is fortunate enough to win a medal or a special award, more than prestige is involved. In the Senior division, Gold Medal winners receive $8,000; Silver Medal winners $5000; Bronze Medal winners $3000; and Best Couple $1000. The Junior Gold Medal winners receive $3000; Silver Medal $2000; Bronze Medal $1000 and the Best Couple $1000. In addition, the winner of the Choreography Award receives $2,500; the Robert Joffrey Award of Merit $800; the Jury Award of Encouragement $500. Various scholarships are also awarded. In case of a tie the winners share the monetary award.

HOUSING

The USA IBC provides and pays for housing and food for each competitor and non-competing partner. In addition, housing and food is provided for dancers winning awards who will be required to participate in the Encore Gala performance on the last day of the competition. Special rates are available for housing and food for the competitors' coaches at Belhaven College.

HOSPITALITY AND HOST FAMILIES

The residents of Jackson welcome the IBC with open arms. Their wholehearted support and hospitality is palpable to the competitors as well as anyone who comes to town for this event. Volunteers provide transportation around the city as well as to and from the airport, production and office assistance, medical services, interpreting and signage. They host parties, are ushers, staff merchandise tables, provide interpreters for foreign visitors; this list goes on and on.

A group called Host Families is one aspect of the Jackson competition that is very much appreciated by all of those attending. Host Families volunteer to be on call for the dancers, faculty, judges or other people involved. These gracious local families provide anything that is needed at any time of the day, from food to Band-Aids to chauffering service.

Ballet Instruction at the Competition

THE INTERNATIONAL DANCE SCHOOL

During its inaugural year the USA IBC became the first international ballet competition to host an International Dance School. The dance classes provide an opportunity for intermediate and advanced level students to study with some of the world's leading teachers and to attend exciting performances. A two-week session is offered for students ages twelve and up at the intermediate and advanced levels who have had a minimum of four consecutive years of ballet training. The curriculum includes ballet technique, pointe and variations, jazz, modern, contemporary and character dance. Additional activities are planned for students' free time.

Some of the well-known teachers who have been on the faculty over the years are Leon Danielian, Gus Giordano, Sophia Golovkina, Robert Joffrey, Bella Lewitzy, Thalia Mara, Richard Englund, Anna-Marie Holmes, Robert Barnett, Peter Pawlyshyn, Francis Roach, Zhanna Dubrovskaya, Marcus Alford, Rhodie Jorgensen, Egon Bischoff, Ekaterina Maximova, Tatiana Legat and Laura Alonso.

© Christopher Jean-Richard

Wu Haiyan (China), Senior gold medalist, at the 2002 USA IBC

95

Teachers' Course

A teachers' workshop is available for professional ballet teachers and those dancers who would like to expand their knowledge of teaching ballet. At the end of each day of this two week course, the participants are free to attend the competition rounds. They are also invited to observe the international guest teachers give morning class to the competitors. Housing is provided at Belhaven College at a nominal charge, or hotels can be recommended by the IBC staff. Teachers bringing students to the school receive discounts on the cost of the course.

Residencies and Other Workshops

Over the years various dance companies have been invited to a residency during the IBC. For two days in 2002, the Gus Giordano Jazz Dance Company of Chicago held a master class, a lecture-demonstration and performed as a part of the IBC evening program. The Paul Taylor Dance Company (in 1998) and the African American Dance Ensemble (in 1994) each offered a demonstration workshop, a master class and a performance. A Pilates workshop was offered free in 2002.

Jackson's Special Features

It is important to note that while other competitions have incorporated some of the special components described below, Thalia Mara insisted that the USA IBC be an educational, truly memorable experience for dancers, judges and the audience. Its special features are:

*   The International Dance School

*   The teacher training program

*   Ancillary exhibits

*   Dancers who have been eliminated may stay and participate in the International Dance School

*   Counselors will discuss the competitors' performances after they have been eliminated, in order to guide them for the future

*   A major ballet or dance company performs as a part of the Opening Ceremony

The Competition Experience

© Hubert Worley

Adrienne Canterna (USA), Junior gold medalist, and Rasta Thomas (USA) Senior gold medalist, at the 1998 USA IBC.

© Christopher Jean-Richard

Danny Tidwell (USA), Junior silver medalist, at the 2002 USA IBC.

DANNY TIDWELL

Danny Tidwell, Junior silver medalist in 2002, had been doing convention competitions, such as Dance Alliance, for a long time before entering the Jackson Competition. He thought he knew what he was getting into due to his other experiences. He had also seen tapes of his partner's sister, Adrienne Canterna, and her partner, Rasta Thomas, when they won the gold medal in 1998. Nevertheless, he said that the experience was "an eye-opener." When he arrived there, he was impressed to see people from all over the world speak the same language through dance. Danny said that his life was changed because it gave him a lot of exposure which ultimately resulted in a job with American Ballet Theatre.

JOSEPH PHILLIPS

The Junior gold medal winner in 2002, Joseph Phillips, now a member of the San Francisco Ballet, says that competing in Jackson was a really great experience for him. "There's no other place where you can get so much exposure. You usually have to go to Paris, London, San Francisco, New York or Boston to audition, but if you come to this competition, those people are all here."

April Ball, Junior silver medalist, and her brother Simon Ball (both of the USA), Junior gold medalist, at the 1994 USA IBC.

Joseph Phillips (USA), Junior gold medalist, at the 2002 USA IBC.

APRIL BALL AND SIMON BALL

April Ball, the Junior silver medalist in 1994, came from a small school in Pennsylvania. She said that if she had been trained in New York, it would have been easier to be seen and possibly discovered. Competing at Jackson gave her the exposure that lead to a job with the Boston Ballet, the Suzanne Farrell Company and later a ballet company in Monte Carlo. Being known as a medalist has also helped when she wanted to take class in other cities. She didn't have to convince people of her worth or promote herself. She also said that because she had to prepare for the competition, she got a lot of personal training and coaching that she would not have normally had. She and her brother, Simon, the Junior gold medal winner that same year, feel that it was a no-lose situation.

Simon adds that he thinks that whether the dancers did well or poorly by judges' standards, that they still walked away with a realization of where they stood, which in his mind can only be positive. He also says that he feels it is very valuable for young people to see other artists from around the world, to which they would never, otherwise, be exposed.

WILLIAM STARRETT

William Starrett, the Senior bronze medal winner at the first USA IBC in 1979 says his career has benefited in numerous ways by his Jackson experience. One of the most important was that Robert Joffrey hired him to be a member of his company. Then every time William would perform with the Joffrey, an announcement would be made that "tonight's performance is being danced by the bronze medal winner, William Starrett."

William Starrett (USA), Senior bronze medalist, at the 1979 USA IBC.

© Hubert Worley

José Carreño (Cuba), City of Jackson Grand Prix winner, and Ana Lobe at the 1990 USA IBC.

When the Joffrey Company had an eight-month layoff because their European tour was cancelled, Bruce Marks invited William to be a guest artist in Boston. Then Patricia Wilde invited him to Pittsburgh. The list goes on, because of the connections he made in Jackson. William ultimately appeared as guest artist with forty different ballet companies.

JOSÉ MANUEL CARREÑO

The highest honor to be granted to a competitor, The City of Jackson Grand Prix, was presented to José Manuel Carreño in 1990 who, at that time, was dancing with the Ballet Nacional de Cuba. This principal dancer, now with American Ballet Theatre, has also danced with the English National Ballet and the Royal Ballet as well as appearing as guest artist with companies around the world since competing in Jackson. He says that the experience was like coming to a great door. Then winning the Grand Prix placed him at the entrance—the gilded door that has led to so many opportunities in his professional life as a world-famous dancer. Even though it wasn't his first experience dancing abroad, he feels that Jackson was the turning point in his career.

Katia Carranza (Mexico), Senior bronze medalist at the 2002 USA IBC.

KATIA CARRANZA AND LUIS SERRANO

Luis Serrano was born in Cuba and studied there for eight years until he was eighteen. He worked with the Ballet Nacional de Cuba for three months before going to Venezuela to dance professionally. In 1994 Luis came to Jackson as a non-competing partner. He liked the experience and decided to compete in 1998, performing only solos and winning the Senior bronze medal. "I wouldn't be dancing in the U.S. if it wasn't for Jackson," he says. The only way Cuban dancers can get a visa to get out of the country is by competing. The staff of the USA IBC helped with all the paperwork and sent letters to the Cuban government, encouraging his participation. Even though he was working in Venezuela at the time, he held a Cuban passport that required he compete as a representative of Cuba. Right now he is a U.S. resident but wants to become a citizen. (He can go back to Cuba to visit his family, but only relatives over sixty years old are allowed to leave Cuba to visit family in the United States). After the first round, Edward Villella, Artistic Director of the Miami City Ballet, offered him a contract, but before the final round, he broke his toe during rehearsal; he had to perform three

Katia Carranza (Mexico), and Luis Serrano (Cuba), at the USA IBC 25th Anniversary Reunion Gala

variations with a broken toe. Against his doctor's advice, he had painkiller shots before each variation in the affected toe to numb the pain, since it was so important to him to finish the competition. He won a bronze medal in the Senior division as well as a job in Miami!

While participating in the 1998 competition, Luis met competitor Katia Carranza, from Mexico. Even though Katia did not win a medal (she got to the final round) she was also hired to dance with the Miami City Ballet as a member of the *corps de ballet*. Like Luis, she feels that the competition changed her life by allowing her to dance in the United States. Soon their lives would not only be changed professionally, but personally. Luis and Katia fell in love and were married. Luis coached his new wife and another company member, Mikhail Ilyin, for the 2002 competition at which they both won bronze medals in the Senior division. In 2004, the three of them were invited to Jackson to participate in the 25th Anniversary Gala Performance. At this time Katia announced that she had recently been promoted to Principal Dancer.

AGNES OAKS AND THOMAS EDUR

"It's a long story starting in Estonia," Tom Edur begins. "We (he and his fiancée, Agnes Oaks) would never have gotten out of the country without a good reason since Estonia was a communist country in 1990." A Finnish friend of their teacher arranged for them to apply to enter the USA IBC through Finland. The application still had to go through Moscow, but if it had gone directly, they would not have been approved—the Russian government was sending only Russian dancers to the competition.

The Estonian Theatre paid for their plane tickets to New York and gave them $100 for spending money. Once they arrived in the United States, they realized that $100 would not take them the rest of the way. Thalia Mara came to the rescue by arranging transportation to Jackson for both of them and their coach.

Besides the Mississippi heat, Tom remembers the wonderful breakfasts offered to the competitors at Belhaven College. With all of these delicious choices before him, he couldn't resist eating them all.

When they entered the competition, Tom and Agnes didn't expect to win; they really just wanted to see the world. In the end, Tom won a Senior bronze medal and together they won the award for Best Couple.

The people of Jackson continually lived up to their reputation for being warm, caring and hospitable. When it was learned that Tom and Agnes would be married when they returned to Estonia, the owner of a chic store in town gave them an expensive wedding

© Hubert Worley

Picture: Agnes Oaks and Thomas Edur (USSR), Senior best couple winners at the 1990 USA IBC.

Katherine Healy (USA) Junior silver medalist at the 1982 USA IBC.

gown. In addition, they were showered with wedding presents. The couple was thrilled and touched by these gestures. It was like a dream! The prize money they won at the competition, between $3500 and $4000, would have been enough for them to live on for two years in Estonia.

Even more importantly, they were offered jobs by members of the jury, and their coach made a contact with the English National Ballet. The job offer from that company was accepted, and when they arrived in London on October 4, 1990, Tom and Agnes felt as if they were still on their honeymoon. "How grateful we are that it all started at the IBC," says Tom. "None of this would have happened without Jackson and Thalia Mara."

KATHERINE HEALY REMEMBERS

Katherine Healy, Junior silver medalist in 1982, has several connections to the USA IBC. While all the winners have been exceptionally talented and well-trained, Katherine stands out for being extraordinary.

Like many American children, she studied more than one subject. Unlike most children, she forged two careers and excelled in both. She began ice skating when she was three years old and at four she began to study dance. In 1981, when she was

twelve, Katherine studied ballet with David Howard at the suggestion of her skating mentor John Curry. There was no question that she was a prodigy in both fields. When asked when she got the idea of entering the competition, she replied that she had studied at the School of American Ballet with 1979 Junior silver medal winner Deirdre Carberry. Deirdre also studied ballet with David in New York. "It looked like a fun thing to do," she remarked.

At that time, she had just finished making a feature film called "Six Weeks" starring Mary Tyler Moore and Dudley Moore. She was required to do a lot of pointe work in the movie, which was a treat since she was still a child. Before that, she had been Marie in New York City Ballet's *Nutcracker* and had also danced in NYCB's *Coppelia* and *Harlequinade*, all priceless experiences. After having the good fortune to be cast in those ballets, she was now anxious to dance in grown-up roles on pointe. Entering the competition gave her the opportunity to study a principal's repertoire. It seemed a natural progression.

A significant moment at the Opening Ceremony of the 1982 USA IBC: Katherine Healy has just carried the torch down the aisle and up to the stage, where she is greeted by a judge, Vera Kirova (USSR) and Robert Joffrey, Chairman of the Jury, who played an important part in the early years of the Competition.

When she applied to the IBC, she was just thirteen years old, and the Junior division, at that time, was for dancers from ages 14 to 19. Fortunately, a special dispensation was made so that she could compete, and, with David Howard as her coach, train for the competition during the spring of 1982.

One of the many advantages of competing was that Katherine was able to see outstanding dancing. During rehearsals she watched other dancers prepare. The dancer who really caught her eye was a young Chinese woman named Wang Qifeng (who had to withdraw because her partner defected—Chinese dancers didn't participate in the competition again until 1990). She had beautiful balances and consecutive double *fouettés*. It had never occurred to Katherine that such things were possible. When she saw this, she said, "Hey, I'm going to do that!" Wang could even do balances that were six counts long, which, again, Katherine didn't know were possible.

Another dancer who influenced her was Janie Parker (gold medal winner in the Senior division and principal dancer with the Houston Ballet for many years) in *The Nutcracker*. "I believe she influenced my *Nutcracker* for the rest of my career. It was just so perfect. Ben Stevenson's version suited her very well. She had those beautiful feet; she had the movement; she had the eyes; she had the expression and her *développé* front was perfect. I watched the video of it over and over and over. Janie was a major influence on me."

Wang Qifeng, special jury award winner, and Lin Jian Wei (both of China), at the 1982 USA IBC.

By 1990 Katherine had graduated from Princeton University magna cum laude. The local Jackson television station invited her to do commentary for their coverage of the Gala that year. Her third trip to Jackson was in 1994. This time, she and José Manuel Carreño performed the *Don Quixote pas de deux* at the Gala.

Ice skating is her current profession. Comparing ballet competitions to those in skating, she said ballet competitions are much longer than skating events so familiar to us from television. "In the Olympics your event is usually over in two or three days. Then you're done and you stay to watch the rest of the athletes. In Jackson you spend more than two weeks being "on" all the time. It's a real challenge to get through it physically and emotionally. If you make it through each round, you have to keep rehearsing every day and keep yourself together emotionally. If a dancer can survive this, he or she can do pretty much anything."

Another comparison she makes between ballet and skating competitions is in the scoring system. She says that in ballet the winners are awarded for a level of achievement. If the judges decide that no one danced on a gold medal level, they won't award it. The jury may award the silver and bronze and give no one a gold. "In skating," she explains, "if somebody gives a bad performance and everybody else is worse, you could still get the gold medal since the top scorer always comes in first. It's much

tougher in ballet because it's more artistic and ephemeral. You can't really quantify it."

Also, in ballet there are no specified technical requirements. In a skating competition, the skater may have to have three combinations with a certain number of triple jumps, a certain number of spins and a number of revolutions on the spin. There are many rules. Katherine says, "In ballet they don't say, 'we need to see three double *pirouettes* and thirty-two *fouettés*.' There are no requirements so you don't know what you have to put in the choreography. How much do you need to do or what's too much? What is over the top? It's all a guess!"

Katherine summarizes: "In ballet, competitions are just an option. You don't have to do them, and most people don't. It's not a rite of passage. It just happened to be very good for me. In ice skating, you have to take part in competitions, but not in ballet. Usually, you train for years, you join a company and you work your way up. And since you don't have to do a competition, the people who do are putting a lot of pressure on themselves. The jury is made up of directors, choreographers and famous dancers that you can't fool. You're putting yourself on the line. It's brave, and it is a baptism by fire because you find out if you can produce when you have to. Taking part opens some doors that might not have opened, so it's a gamble worth taking, but it's pretty tough. Ballet is not set up like a sport where you have to compete. It's just a very nice thing to be able to do."

AUDIENCES

Senior bronze medal winner in 2002, Mikhail Ilyin, a member of the Miami City Ballet, has an interesting insight. He sees a great advantage for audience members of ballet competitions, because they get to see dancers from all over the world who represent different styles and companies. Misha feels something incredible happens to a person when he or she becomes a ballet enthusiast. "In Greek theatre it is said that the audience leaves the theater with beautiful thoughts that enable them to make beautiful things themselves. Surrounded by beauty, you create beauty."

COACHES

No matter how much innate talent a dancer possesses, he or she must still be taught and guided by experts. Below are stories of exceptional commitment on the part of the coaches.

Joseph Phillips, Junior Gold Medal winner in 2002, has also been a medalist in several other competitions. His coach, Stanislav Issaev, who he described as being like a father, prepared him for all of them at no charge. Joseph trained for nearly five years, and the cost of that private coaching would have added up to a great deal of money.

Jana Kurova (Czechoslovakia), Senior silver medal winner (and Senior best couple winner with Ludomir Kafka),Deirdre Carberry (USA), Junior silver medal winner, and Jessica Funt (USA), Junior silver medal winner (and Junior best couple winner with Koenraad Onzia of Belgium), at the 1979 USA IBC

Simon Ball states, "my major influence and mentor was the teacher that prepared me for Jackson. His name is Roberto Munoz. He is now the head of the school at Pittsburgh Ballet Theatre. He is just an amazing guy who did more than just train us (Simon and his sister, April Ball) for ballet. He inspired us to put value into what we were doing and taught us ballet history."

Three coaches, Loipa Araujo, Lazaro Carreño and Laura Alonso, were selected by the Ballet Nacional de Cuba to prepare José Manuel Carreño for the competition. He felt very fortunate to be under the tutelage of these great people.

Sarah Lamb says that she wanted to come to the competition because it would enable her to work with her coach intensively on different variations that are part of the company's repertoire. Her coach, Tatiana Nicolaevna Legat, is the granddaughter of Nicholas Legat who was Nijinsky's teacher. "She has an incredible wealth of knowledge and is a genius, so to be able to work with her is just a gift. On top of that, she donated all of her time. She wouldn't take any money from me. It's the Russian way; they do it for the art, not money. What she has given me has been out of love. I could never repay her. It would be tens of thousands of dollars, I'm sure."

Advice from Medalists to Future Competitors

RASTA THOMAS

Rasta Thomas was already an experienced competition dancer when he entered the USA IBC in 1998 at seventeen. He had already won the special jury prize at the Paris International Competition in 1994 and a Junior gold medal at Varna in 1996 before winning a Senior gold medal in Jackson. His advice to those considering entering the competition is to only perform what you do well. He says it's good to rehearse a more difficult variation, but when it comes to performing, don't attempt something you rarely do well. For example, some dancers try to do multiple pirouettes when it would be better to have done two, three or four. It's best to have the audience think that you would have done more if there had been more music, rather than to fall attempting five or six.

For the girl who doesn't have the best physique for ballet, Rasta recommends wearing a long tutu, since a short skirt is far more revealing. Also, the repertoire should be chosen carefully; ideally, it should highlight the dancer's strengths. Choosing a wonderful partner is of utmost importance, says Rasta. He was fortunate to have had Adrienne Canterna, a dancer with whom he grew up, as his partner. That year she won a gold medal, as well, in the Junior division.

Rasta believes that you can't enter a competition in the hope of winning money. You could do it for the medal, you do it to keep in shape, but he thinks you need to do it just because you really love to dance. "One of my mentors says, 'dance like the dancer you want to become. Don't dance like the dancer you are today—dance like you want to dance and the way you want to be remembered.'"

JOSÉ MANUEL CARREÑO

Combining technique and passion for dance in a perfect, even mix is the advice that José Manuel Carreño has for young dancers whether entering a competition or not. He calls it having equilibrium. José says, "anyone who decides to make his or her body a vehicle to communicate, to express feelings and ideas must achieve that balance. Virtuosos without a soul are excellent acrobats. Ballet is the soul in motion."

SARAH LAMB

Sarah Lamb advises future competitors to stay as calm as possible. She remembers warming up in a hallway before going onstage and thinking, "I could just walk out the back exit door now." She adds, "I find myself having random thoughts: is my pinky in the right place? Is my foot turned out enough? Is my eyelash on the right angle? Dance is such minutia that it really becomes difficult. Don't get caught up in the details. Just try to relax and dance."

DANIEL TIDWELL

Danny Tidwell thinks the competition works better for Seniors than for Juniors. He believes that if he had been older, he would have taken the opportunity to develop relationships with others at the competition, and, instead of just dancing and exploring his art, he was focused on competing.

Sarah Lamb (USA) at the USA IBC 25th Anniversary Reunion Gala

© Alexander Skalij

JOSEPH PHILLIPS

Even when great opportunities are presented, Joseph Phillips, now a member of the San Francisco Ballet, feels it's best to finish high school before moving on to a professional career. After winning the gold medal in 2002, he returned home to finish high school before looking for a job. After graduation, he sent a video along with his résumé to SFB. On the résumé was his Jackson credit, which he said he knows made a difference.

KATHERINE HEALY

"Be sure to drink a lot of liquids and eat a well-balanced diet to keep your body healthy and strong," is Katherine Healy's advice. Summer heat in the South is intense, and it's dangerous to get dehydrated. She also advises not to become completely dependent on your coach. "Take what you need, put it inside yourself and learn how to use it so that later you won't need his or her physical presence. It is not good to become so emotionally attached that you can't work without a coach."

Thalia Mara (1911-2003)

Thalia Mara in Romance (Fokine), 1938.
Pastel portrait by the Spanish court painter Enrique Dorda

Born Elizabeth Simmons on June 28, 1911 in Chicago, Thalia was the daughter of Russian immigrants named Semyonov (which was changed to "Simmons" in America).

Thalia made her ballet debut on a Chicago vaudeville stage at the age of eleven and was enthralled with performing the first time the curtain went up. She grew from a vaudeville mini-star to an accomplished ballerina under the direction of such ballet masters as Adolph Bolm, Olga Preobrajenska, Nicolas Legat and Michel Fokine. (Virtually all of her training was from Diaghilev-era icons of the Russian School.)

Thalia performing in the troupe of her first teacher, Miss Butler.

Thalia repeatedly paid tribute to her famous teacher, Olga Preobrajenska. She often said "Preobrajenska's great gift as a teacher was her intelligence and ability to *analyze*, not only the technique but also those refined details that developed artistry and the individual expressiveness of each of her students." "Preo" was able to transfer to her charges all those subtle qualities that distinguished her as a performer. In addition to her technical perfection, she was noted for her grace, elegance, dignity, her soaring leaps and a rare musicality... a "poetess of dance." She stressed the importance of dancing the soul. In class she was a rigid disciplinarian, maintained great authority, and commanded absolute attention. However, she also showed infinite compassion and kindness and lavished great attention on those students who were especially receptive. Preobrajenska taught the principles of the Russian School and incorporated a strong influence of the Cecchetti School. Even after she achieved the status of prima ballerina, she sought out Enrico Cecchetti as a teacher. The Russian School developed students as expressive artists (not just as technicians) by stressing use of the upper body. "Dance with your head, your eyes, *mes enfants*," she said. The Cecchetti School intensified the drive for more strength, vigor and brilliance of technique.

"It's a very deep approach to ballet," Thalia once explained. "You are dancing the music—you are not dancing to the music. You dance the minute details of the character." To Thalia, ballet was pure expression of life. "Ballet is not nearly as physical as it is spiritual, more in the mind," she said. "To achieve the mastery of your body, you have to meet the most rigid disciplines...and through that, your body becomes free. Dance is the only art form in which an artist himself becomes a work of art."

After vaudeville, fourteen-year-old Thalia became a full member of both the Chicago Opera Ballet under Bolm's direction and the Ravinia Park Opera Ballet under Ruth Page. At that time (the 1920s), because an American school of ballet had not yet developed, Thalia, at sixteen, went to Paris to learn ballet at its source where she studied classical ballet and character dance with Preobrajenska and Legat.

A performance of the Ballet Suédois de Carina Ari in Montreux, Switzerland (the town is in the background). Thalia is the soloist at left of center.

Thalia soon rose to prominence as a soloist with *Ballet Suédois de Carina Ari* and *L'Opéra Privé de Paris*, touring France and the rest of Europe. While in Paris, she met dancer Arthur Mahoney, whom she married eleven years later. Arthur had traveled to Paris from Boston to study ballet and performed as one of the *caballeros* in the premiere of the famous *Bolero*. The dancer Ida Rubenstein had commissioned Maurice Ravel to write the music for her, and hired Nijinska as the choreographer.

In 1929 Thalia and Arthur embarked on a tour through Europe, South America and the United States with *L'Opéra Privé de Paris*. While in this company Thalia danced for the first time under the direction of the great master Michel Fokine, performing in one of the first productions of his ballet *Prince Igor*.

Returning to the United States and settling in New York, Thalia took a job with the Capitol Theater as one of the Chester Hale Girls. She felt fortunate to have a job as a dancer— it was at the height of the Great Depression. She later said she took the job because "I had to eat." Even though times were tough, Thalia, obviously amused, would later relate, "We did every type of dancing imaginable—ballet, jazz, character dancing; even ballet on roller skates." Apparently she valued her job as a Chester Hale Girl enough to risk her life for it because, on one occasion, she did just that. In the era before television, promoters dreamed up

stunts so that their clients would appear in newsreels shown at movie houses.

"We had an aggressive promoter," Thalia recalled. "It occurred to her that if we could dance in front of the spire of the newly-built Chrysler Building, it would be a surefire newsreel item." Subsequently, a 16' x 16' platform without safety rails was rigged next to the towering spire fifty-seven stories over the street below. When the sixteen Chester Hale Girls refused to dance in this perilous situation, it was decided that half of them should do it, giving each girl a little more than a foot of space.

A photograph of Thalia inscribed "For Arthur, Remember Elizabeth, Buenos Aires, 1929." (Elizabeth Simmons, at eighteen, had not yet changed her name to Thalia Mara.)

116

"Of course, it turned out to be my half of the line," she remembered. And because she was the tiniest, she was perched on the end. What made things even more difficult were the little masks the dancers wore as part of their costumes. On top of that it was a windy day in March. The performance went on, and the newsreel cameras were there to record the moment. Thalia's knees became weak, even years later, at the thought of this performance.

Thalia became a regular ballet soloist at Radio City Music Hall, which opened December 27, 1932. She performed from early morning to 11 o'clock in the evening seven days a week, four shows a day except on holidays, when she did five. She also danced at the Roxy Theater and in several Broadway shows including *The Great Waltz*, an operetta about the Johann Strausses, father and son. Arthur performed as a soloist at the Music Hall including the lead in a performance staged by Vincente Minnelli called *The Sun King*.

Thalia and Arthur Mahoney at Radio City Music Hall.

Backstage at the Lewisohn Stadium in New York, Thalia, in costume for The Fokine American Ballet Company's Scheherazade with the great Michel Fokine (in the background).

While she was in her early 20's, she changed her name from Elizabeth Simmons to the stage and legal name of "Thalia" (the Greek muse of humor) "Mara" (a family name) to attract more stage work. Her mother and friends helped her choose the name.

In the 1930s she became a soloist in New York's Fokine Ballet just as American ballet began to come of age. While Thalia and Arthur Mahoney had careers independent of each other, they also performed as a pair. They developed concert programs showing various styles of dance with ballet as the core. In 1937 they toured as concert artists across the United States and Canada performing ballet, flamenco, jazz and court dances of the seventeenth and eighteenth centuries. This was the great jazz era and Arthur, who choreographed for them both, frequented the jazz clubs in Harlem, especially the Savoy, where Fats Waller played the piano. It was here that he learned the Lindy Hop. Thalia and Arthur brought it to the stage, incorporating it into their program finale. They called it the twentieth century minuet.

Thalia performing solo concert dances (ballet and flamenco) during one of the U.S. tours, showing her ability to excel in demanding and different kinds of dancing.

They both were accomplished flamenco artists, performing as a couple in *Quadra Flamenco* and in complete flamenco programs with a full company of dancers. José Greco, who popularized flamenco in the United States, was their student.

As Thalia Mara became more involved with the teaching and directing aspects of her art, she became a dedicated advocate for raising standards of ballet instruction. She established the Ballet Repertory Guild, a training and certifying organization for teachers of ballet; its mission was to set dance teaching standards in America. She served as its president from 1951 to 1963.

In 1962, she founded and directed the National Academy of Ballet in New York. It was modeled after the state-supported

Thalia and Arthur performing flamenco,

performing a jazz dance,

in the demi-caractère dance Beau Danube (Massine).

schools that existed in Europe and Russia. Elementary and high school students (from grades four through twelve) received a complete academic education with extensive training in the performing arts. Serving on its advisory board were Sol Hurok and Senators Jacob Javits and Robert F. Kennedy. It became one of two such accredited schools in the United States and the forerunner of schools of its type in the United States. Thalia's National Academy graduates became principal dancers in such renowned companies as American Ballet Theatre, Joffrey Ballet, San Francisco Ballet, Stuttgart Ballet and the Bavarian State Opera Ballet in Munich. Although the concept gained acceptance, funding waned and the school closed in the early 1970s.

Thalia and Arthur in an 18th century court dance.

With their parrot, Pepo, acquired in South America. Pepo was with Thalia for forty-five years.

JOLINDA MENENDEZ REMEMBERS THE NATIONAL ACADEMY OF BALLET

At the age of eight Jolinda came from Trinidad to audition for The National Academy of Ballet at the insistence of her local teacher. "Basically, I ended up being with Miss Mara from the age of nine until I graduated from high school. My mother took me to her and entrusted me to her full care. It was a big step—coming to New York at such a young age to begin living my life toward the goal of becoming a ballerina. Little did I know that Miss Mara would be more than a teacher. She saw me grow up and nurtured me as a little girl. I even lived in her home until the school had dormitories. I was around her most of the time during those formative years. Discipline, determination and commitment were only a few of the qualities that were the backbone of her school. Without the love and, above all, the spiritual guidance that she instilled in me, I would not have been prepared for life."

Jolinda went on to a professional career with American Ballet Theatre and with companies in Europe. She now teaches at Tisch School of the Arts of New York University, as well as guest-teaches and coaches dancers all over the world.

A class of lower school students (ages eight to thirteen) at the National Academy of Ballet.

Guest teacher Asaf Messerer (Director of the Bolshoi Ballet) presented flowers by student Jolinda Menendez.

During her decades of teaching, Thalia built an international reputation as a ballet educator. She became the author of a dozen books including several ballet textbooks for dance students and teachers published in the United States and England. They have been translated into German, Spanish, Arabic and Japanese.

Thalia left New York for Jackson, Mississippi, in 1975 when she was hired to be artistic director of the Jackson Ballet. Her mission and intention was to bring the company to a national level.

Jolinda Menendez, Clark Tippet and Michael Wasmund (at about twelve years old) reheasing at N.A.B.

Jolinda Menendez and Clark Tippet (at fifteen) coached by Anton Dolin in Swan Lake pas de deux at N.A.B.

By 1979 it was a fully professional company of twenty four dancers. Some of the company and students from its ballet school moved on to notable companies such as the Berlin Opera Ballet and the New York City Ballet. In 1981, due to the lack of fiscal and managerial support to maintain the company's high standards, Thalia resigned.

Thalia rehearsing with the Jackson Ballet Company.

After moving to Mississippi, Thalia became involved in many projects, but the one that has left the most lasting mark is the USA International Ballet Competition. As she struggled to bring it to Jackson, she remembered, "People thought I was crazy!" Nevertheless, by her determination and through an act of Congress, Jackson was named the official USA home of the IBC. To show its appreciation, the City Council renamed the Jackson Municipal Auditorium Thalia Mara Hall. She served as its artistic director from 1986 through the fifth competition in 1994.

In 1991 she founded the Thalia Mara Arts International Foundation with the mission to preserve, nurture and advance the education, understanding and love of the arts in all manifestations. Foundation projects have included providing scholarships for the training of teachers at the IBC's dance school, spearheading the 1992 Mississippi Homecoming that celebrated 175 years of statehood, presenting the 1997 Yamaha International Piano Competition winners' concert, and in 1999 launching the World Performance Series.

During her Jackson career, she was guest teacher for many U.S. ballet companies and workshops. In addition, she served as a consultant and judge for the first Alicia Alonso International Dance Competition in Havana, Cuba, the International Concours de Ballet in Tokyo, the Japan Ballet and

Thalia's creation, the Jackson Ballet Company, in Les Sylphides (above) and Bolero (below right).

Modern Dance Competitions in Nagoya, the National Ballet Company in Egypt and the Mexican National Ballet competitions.

On opening night of the seventh International Ballet Competition in 2002, Thalia was presented with a Lifetime Achievement Award and a gold medal for her long career in the arts. As she accepted the award, she was surrounded by her colleagues and friends and hundreds of red roses.

On October 8, 2003, at the age of ninety-two, Thalia Mara passed away, ending a remarkable life of performing, teaching, directing and nurturing the arts.

Sue Lobrano, Executive Director of USA IBC, Thalia Mara, and Bruce Marks, USA IBC Jury Chairman at the 2002 Competition.

Authors and Contributors

Authors

Thalia Mara
Thalia Mara was artistic director of the USA International Ballet Competition; made her ballet debut at the age of eleven, and by fourteen was a full member of the Chicago Opera Ballet under the direction of Adolph Bolm. In Paris she studied under the legendary Nicholas Legat and Olga Preobrajenska, soon rising to prominence as soloist with the Ballet Suédois de Carina Ari and later with the Michel Fokine Ballet in New York. With her husband she founded the School of Dance Arts at Carnegie Hall and the School of Ballet Repertory. Thalia taught at New York's High School of the Performing Arts, then in 1965 founded and directed the National Academy of Ballet.

In 1976, at the age of 65, Thalia moved to Jackson, Mississippi, where she created the Jackson Ballet and established Jackson as the host of the USA International Ballet Competition in 1979, serving as its Artistic Director through 1994.

Janice Barringer
Janice Barringer teaches, choreographs, and lectures in the United States, Canada, and China and writes for many dance magazines. She has been spotlighted in the PBS Dance in America series, and she has been on the faculty of the American Dance Center, Ballet Hispanico, Harkness House, and STEPS on Broadway. She is coauthor of *The Pointe Book, Second Edition.*

Contributors

Leanne Mahoney

Leanne Mahoney, contributor to the section of this book entitled *Thalia Mara* (1911-2003), is Thalia Mara's niece. A graduate of Pratt Institute, she has had a distinguished career as a costume designer and costumer. Among her many credits: she was involved in productions at the Metropolitan Opera, American Ballet Theatre, The Joffrey Ballet, The San Francisco Ballet and Opera as well as original productions of *Camelot, Fiddler On the Roof* and Bob Fosse's *Dancin'*. She also worked in association with designers Willa Kim, Tony Walton and Michael Annals. From 1969-1998 she was Costume Director for the much acclaimed Santa Fe Opera.

Leslie R. Myers

Contributor to *Thalia Mara (1911-2003)*, journalist Leslie R. Myers of Jackson, Mississippi was a dance critic for seventeen years and the only critic in the world to cover the first five USA International Ballet Competitions in Jackson. She was Chairman of Dance Critics for the first Alicia Alonso International Dance Competition in Havana, Cuba, and presented its Spirit of Dance award. A graduate of University of Missouri—Columbia School of Journalism, her articles have appeared in newspapers as well as *Dance Magazine, Opera Canada, Opera London* and *W*.

Rosalie O'Connor

The photographs of Sarah Lamb throughout Part I were taken by Rosalie O'Connor. During the last six years of her fifteen-year career as a dancer with American Ballet Theatre she began to photograph other dancers in the company. In 2002 she made the transition to full-time photographer. Her photographs have been published both nationally and internationally in prominent publications. She also has been the subject of articles, most notably Jennifer Dunning's profile of her in *The New York Times*. She has recently released a calendar and her first book, both featuring dancers of ABT.

Sarah Lamb

Sarah Lamb, the subject of the photographs in Part I, trained at The Boston Ballet School. In 1998 she was a Presidential Scholar in the Arts and was awarded a gold medal by President Clinton. With Madame Tatiana Nicolaevna Legat as her coach she won silver medals at the USA IBC, the sixth New York City IBC and the IBC in Nagoya, Japan. In 1998 she joined The Boston Ballet, was promoted to Soloist in 2001 and Principal in 2003. In August of 2004 Sarah joined London's Royal Ballet as a First Soloist.

Other Books and Videos from
Princeton Book Company, Publishers,
for students and parents

Bibliography

Mara, Thalia. *Steps in Ballet.*

_____. *The Language of Ballet: A Dictionary.*

Barringer; Janice and Sarah Schlesinger. *The Pointe Book: Shoes, Technique and Training, second edition*

Whitehill, Angela and William Noble. *The Parents Book of Ballet: Answers to Critical Questions About the Care and Development of Young Dancers, 2nd Edition.*

_____. *The Nutcracker Backstage: The Story and The Magic.*

Lihs, Harriet R. *Appreciating Dance: A Guide to the World's Liveliest Art, 3rd Edition.*

Newman, Barbara. *Sadler's Wells Royal Ballet Swan Lake.* London: Dance Books Ltd.

Harrison, Mary Kent. *How to Dress Dancers: Costuming Techniques for Dance.*

Spilken, Terry L., M.D. *The Dancer's Foot Book.*

Chmelar, Robin and Sally S. Fitt. *Diet for Dancers: A Complete Guide to Nutrition and Weight Control.*

Videography

Ballet 101 Series:
Ballet 101; Ballet 201; Ballet 101 & 201, Combinations 1; Ballet 101 & 201, Combinations 2. With Angela Russ; based on the syllabus of the University of California at Irvine
each approx. 50 minutes, color.

Zena Rommett Floor-Barre & Ballet Technique for Young Dancers with Sarah Cunningham
35 minutes, color.

My First Pointe Shoes with Michelle Benash
25 minutes, color.

Simply Ballet: An Easy-to-Follow Class for Beginners with Michelle Benash
55 minutes, color.

Ballet Class for Beginners with David Howard
40 minutes, color.

Step into Ballet with Wayne Sleep of the Royal Ballet
50 minutes, color.

The Children of Theatre Street (The Kirov Ballet School) narrated by Princess Grace of Monaco
92 minutes, color.

Videography (continued)

Cinderella, A Ballet in Three Acts
with Antoinette Sibley, Anthony Dowell and the Royal Ballet
Choreography by Ashton, Music by Prokofiev
102 minutes, color.

The Nutcracker
with Ekaterina Maximova, Vladimir Vasiliev and The Bolshoi Ballet
Choreography by Grigorovich, Music by Tchaikovsky
100 minutes, color.

The Nutcracker
with Merle Park, Rudolf Nureyev and The Royal Ballet
Choreography by Nureyev, Music by Tchaikovsky
100 minutes, color.

The Sleeping Beauty, A Ballet in Three Acts
with Viviana Durante, Anthony Dowell and
The Royal Ballet Covent Garden
Choreography by Petipa, Ashton and MacMillan, Music by Tchaikovsky
132 minutes, color.

The Sleeping Beauty
with Christine Walsh, David Ashmole and The Australian Ballet
Choreography by Petipa, Music by Tchaikovsky
134 minutes, color.

The Sleeping Beauty
with Altynai Asylmuratova, Konstantin Zaklinsky and The Kirov Ballet
Choreography by Petipa, Music by Tchaikovsky
160 minutes, color.

I'm A Ballerina Now with Rosemary Boross
and students of the Red Bank Dance Academy
40 minutes, color.

DVDs

Beginner & Lower Intermediate Pointe Classes With Janice Barringer
For teachers and students
62 minutes, color.

Intermediate-Advanced Ballet Center With Janice Barringer
For teachers and students
37 minutes, color.

Cinderella, A Ballet in Three Acts
with Antoinette Sibley, Anthony Dowell and the Royal Ballet
Choreography by Ashton, Music by Prokofiev
102 minutes, color.

The Nutcracker
with Maximova, Vasiliev and The Bolshoi Ballet
Choreography by Grigorovich, Music by Tchaikovsky
100 minutes, color.

The Sleeping Beauty, A Ballet in Three Acts
with Durante, Dowell and The Royal Ballet Covent Garden
Choreography by Petipa, Ashton and Macmillan, Music by Tchaikovsky.

Compact Disc

Music for Ballet Class with Olga Meyer, Pianist